BACK TO PATRIARCHY

Daniel Amńeus

BACK TO PATRIARCHY

BACK TO PATRIARCHY

Daniel Amńeus

BACK TO PATRIARCHY

ARLINGTON HOUSE·PUBLISHERS
NEW ROCHELLE, NEW YORK

Library of Congress Cataloging in Publication Data

Amneus, Daniel.
    Back to patriarchy.

    Bibliography: p.
    Includes index.
    1. Sex   role.   2. Equality.   3. Feminism—United
States.   4. Men—United   States.   5. Family—United
States.   I. Title.
HQ1075.A46   301.41   78-27715
ISBN 0-87000-436-0

FOR
PAUL AND PAMELA

Thanks To

Dr. Carlo Abruzzese, Myron Balych, Richard Band, Steve Barnes, Elizabeth Breedlove, George Doppler, R. F. Doyle, Rosalee Johnson, Norm Kopp, Don Lamb, Dave Morrow, Nillo Piccinin, Dr. Gerald Silver, Bob Starkman.

And To The Following
Whose Books Are Cited
Throughout This Work

Avon Books, publisher of Susan Ross's *The Rights of Women*, N.Y., 1974 and of Kate Millet's *Sexual Politics*, 1969; Basic Books, N.Y., publisher of Nathan Glazer's *Affirmative Discrimination: Ethnic Inequality and Public Policy*, 1975; Coward, McCann, and Geoghagan, Berkley Publishing Company, publisher of the *New Women's Survival Catalogue*; Diana Press, publisher of *Lesbianism in the Women's Movement*, Baltimore, 1975; Doubleday, publisher of Charles Metz's *Divorce and Custody for Men*, N.Y., 1968; *Everybody's Money*; *The Family Circle*: Glencoe Press, publisher of E. Adams and L. Briscoe's *Up Against The Wall, Mother*, Beverly Hills, 1971; Grune and Stratton, publisher of Bergler and Kroger, *Kinsey's Myth of Female Sexuality*; Harper and Row, publisher of Birgitta Linner's *Sex and Society in Sweden*, N.Y., 1967, F. Lundberg and M. Farnham *Modern Woman: The Lost Sex*, 1947, and of B. and T. Roszak's *Masculine/Feminine*, 1969; Holbrook Press, publisher of J. Gazell's *Youth, Crime and Society*, Boston, 1973; *The Humanist*, in which Alice Rossi's "Sex Equality: The Beginning of Ideology" was originally published (Sept./Oct., 1969); Indiana University's Institute for Sex Research, Inc., publisher of Kinsey's *Sexual Behavior in the Human Male*, 1948; Alfred Knopf- Random House, publisher of L. Fuchs's *Family Matters*, N.Y., 1972, Michael Korda's *Male Chauvinism: How*

It Works, 1975, and H. L. Mencken's *In Defense of Women*, 1922; Know, Inc., Pittsburgh, Pa., publisher of Roberta Greene's *Till Divorce Do You Part*, 2nd ed., 1972; *The Los Angeles Free Press*, in which the quote from "Off Dr. Bieber" originally appeared, 14 August 1970; *The Los Angeles Times*; McGraw-Hill Book Co., publisher of Germaine Greer's *The Female Eunuch*, N.Y., Bantam Books, 1970, F. Howe's *Women and the Power to Change*, 1975, and C. A. Tripp's *The Homosexual Matrix*, 1975; David McKay, Co., publisher of Konrad Kellen and Margaret Carpenter's *The Coming Age of Woman Power*, 1972; Macmillan Publishing Co., publishers of Goldstein, Freud and Solnit's *Beyond the Best Interests of the Child:* Manor Books, publisher of Jeanne Cambrai's *Once Is Enough*, N.Y., 1974; The Men's Rights Association and M.E.N. International (Men's Equality Now), publishers of *M.E.N.* (Formerly *The Liberator*), a monthly publication of the Men's Rights Coalition: address Box 189, Forest Lake, Minn. 55025; Meridian Books, publishers of R. Benedict's *The Chrysanthemum and the Sword*, N.Y., 1967; William Morrow and Co., publishers of Steven Goldberg's *The Inevitability of Patriarchy*, N.Y., 1973; *The New York Times* for permission to quote from the Betty Friedan article published in the *New York Times Magazine*, 4 March 1973; W. W. Norton, publisher of Arno Karlen's *Sexuality and Homosexuality*, 1971; Olympia Press, publishers of Valarie Solana's *Scum Manifesto*, N.Y., 1968; Open Court Publishing Co., publisher of George Roche's *The Balancing Act*, LaSalle, Ill., 1974; Pathfinder Press, publishers of Linda Jenness's *Affirmative Action vs. Seniority*, N.Y., 1975, and Betsy Stone's *Sisterhood Is Powerful*, 1970; Poor Richard's Press, publisher of R. F. Doyle's *The Rape of the Male* (now sold by World Wide Book Service, 251 3rd Ave., New York, N.Y. 10010); Porter Sargent, Boston, Mass., publisher of Pitirim Sorokin's *The American Sex Revolution*, 1956, and B. Malinowski and Robert Briffault's *Marriage, Past and Present*, 1932; G. P. Putnam's Sons, *The First Sex* by Elizabeth Gould Davis, N.Y. 1971; Praeger Publishers, publisher of Elizabeth Friar Williams's *Notes of a Feminist Therapist*, N.Y., 1976; Prentice-Hall, Englewood Cliffs, N.J., publisher of David Loovis's *Straight Answers about Homosexuality for Straight Readers*, 1977; S.B.O.N.R. Publishing House,

London, Ont., publisher of Ivan Kurganov's *Women in the USSR*, 1971; St. Martin's Press, publisher of Adelstein and Paval's *Women's Liberation*, N.Y., 1972; Texas Eagle Forum, publisher of Vicki Frierson and Ruthanne Garlock's *Christian Be Watchful*, Dallas, Texas, n.d.; *The Other Woman;* The University of Chicago Press, publisher of F. A. Hayek's *John Stuart Mill and Harriet Taylor*, 1951; The University of Minnesota Press, publisher of S. Hathaway and E. Monachesi's *Adolescent Personality and Behavior*, Minneapolis, Minn., 1963: The University of Pittsburgh Press, publisher of *Female and Male in Latin America: Essays*, ed. Ann Pescatello, 1973, from which the selection from E. Stevens is quoted by permission; Weybright and Talley, publisher of Neil Elliott's *Sensuality in Scandinavia*, N.Y., 1970.

CONTENTS

I

Introduction

The changes necessary to bring about equality were, and still are, very revolutionary
indeed. They involve a sex-role revolution for
men and women which will restructure all
our institutions: child rearing, education,
marriage, the family, medicine, work, politics, the ecomony, religion, psychological
theory, human sexuality, morality and the
very evolution of the race.
                                    —Betty Friedan

By Castor! It's our own fault! We've pampered and spoiled them!
                                    —Aristophanes

FEMINISM CAN BE usefully studied in either of two ways—as a
disease for which there is no known cure, or as a cure for
which there is no known disease. The present book attempts
to examine it in both ways, on the one hand to see it as a mani-
festation of the ineradicable human love of power, which, as
Hazlitt said, is merely another name for the love of mischief,
a love too deeply embedded in our creatureliness to be exor-
cised, though its effects can be greatly palliated; on the other
hand to examine the egregious propaganda in which the
feminists complain of what they affect to call male spermatic
oppression, oppression which it is the purpose of these
ladies to terminate.

Complaints of the feminists are so familiar that readers
scarcely need to be reminded of them: women earn little more
than half of what men earn; they do most of what they deem
society's drudgery; they are a colonialized and exploited
class; they have been socialized into feeling dependent on
men; they are victimized by merchants and manufacturers
who direct three-quarters of their advertising towards them;

they are separated from one another so that they cannot unite to fight their oppression; they have been stunted; they are trapped; marriage is a ghetto, "the great scourge"; women are victims of discrimination by the law; they are treated as mere "children of a larger growth"; their history has been suppressed; they have been made slaves and then condemned for being servile; they are exploited as cheap labor, domestic servants, and breeders; their humanity is denied; they are subjected to physical violence; they suffer dolorously from "the problem that has no name"; they have been trapped for life with a contract written for the benefit of men; they are denied status or they derive what status they have from their fathers or their husbands; only a single woman is found in the Senate and not one on the Supreme Court; they are expected to be nurses while their brothers are encouraged to be doctors; they are victimized by wars that are made by men; socialization and education have prevented them from even being aware of their own oppression, and some of them even believe themselves to be pampered and privileged creatures; they are stereotyped as either Madonnas and Moms or as whores, witches, and castrators; they have been brought up to suppose that patriarchy is the natural order of human society rather than (as has now been explained by feminist scholars such as Helen Diner, Evelyn Reed, and Elizabeth Gould Davis) a relatively modern development; they have been brainwashed by a system of chivalry designed to facilitate their exploitation and oppression; they are "the other," men alone being "truly free existents." They have been excluded from the awesome dignity of the priesthood and stigmatized as sensual temptresses. They are told that they are responsible for bringing sin into the world. They have been bought and sold like chattel. Their children have been taken from them. They have been denied control over their own earnings. They have been denied the right to have abortions, the right to control their own bodies. They are represented in literature and the arts as passive, nurturant, and dependent, whereas males are represented as active, heroic, achieving. They have been induced to bind and cripple their feet; to constrict their waists with cruel corsets; to grow their fingernails to enormous lengths, like those of Chinese mandarins, and then to paint them with garish lacquers; to have their

14

ears pierced, their hair dyed, frizzed, crimped, and curled with hot and expensive equipment and then sprayed with perfumed aerosols that enrich manufacturers at their expense. They have been persuaded to smear their eyelids with antimony like Jezebel; to anoint their bodies with chemicals, lotions, and unguents; and to cover them with powders and perfumes—all for the purpose of arousing and enflaming the passions of lustful men, who then use and exploit them as sex objects. They have been made into mere parasitic ornaments to gratify the vanity of husbands.

A sad litany. Who that can feel the dint of pity will fail to sympathize and compassionate with these wretched and delicate creatures? Who?

And yet there is one thing that is worse than being a woman, and that is being a man. And there is one thing that is worse than being an ordinary male, and that is being an American male, surely the most exploited, even if not the most degraded and impoverished human who ever lived. No Gibeonites ever hewed wood and drew water as the American male hews and draws. No pyramid-builder, straining his shoulder against the rope; no *Landbauer*, crumpling his hat and bowing under the monocled eye of his *Junker*; no fellah, toiling endlessly at his shadouf—none, none, was ever host to so many parasites, was ever so exploited as the American male.

And this exploitation has been borne with a docility that would be incredible if it were less ubiquitously visible—the docility that has made possible such Anglo-Saxon enterprises as the Charge of the Light Brigade, the Battle of the Somme, the Income Tax, the Vietnam War, and the American matriarchy—a docility surpassing even that of such tractable species as asses, merino sheep, and Irish Catholics, and resembling that of those birds on uninhabited islands of whom travelers' tales record that they will suffer themselves to be approached, to be lifted from their perches, and to be wrung by the neck without so much as attempting flight, offering resistance, or uttering a murmur of protest.

It is the thesis of the present book that this docility has gone too far, that the American male has become a mock and a byword and a shaking of the head to the nations, and that we must superimpose a benign and enlightened patriarchalism

15

upon the chaos and fatuity with which we see ourselves surrounded. We must purge society, government, and our families of the cancer of feminism; reform our divorce laws; extrude the rabble of lawyers, legislators, judges, social and welfare workers, psychologists, counselors, court investigators, beadles, bumbles, and bureaucrats from our lives; and once again permit fathers to be the heads of the families. We must abolish alimony and child-support payments in cases of divorce and place the children of divorce in the custody of their natural providers and protectors, their fathers. We must confute the errorists in the feminist camp and their house-males in academe and in government who earn their brownie points and their salaries by sucking and nuzzling around the fringes of the feminist movement and telling these pampered elitists how oppressed they are. We must break up the menacing alliance between feminists and the ever-increasing number of father-substitutes in the bureaucracies dealing with juvenile delinquency, social work, welfare, family law, day care, and so forth—all with a vested interest in the continuing disintegration of the family, a disintegration that has created most of their jobs.

The family in our society, ground between the upper millstone of feminism and the lower millstone of our divorce laws, is under too much pressure, and this pressure must be reduced by the abolition of alimony and child-support payments as they are now imposed in cases of divorce.

The attack on the family by the legal profession and the feminist movement is the most serious problem facing our society today; but other parts of the feminist program are also very serious—affirmative action, demands for free child care, the abolition of the rational socialization of children. The first problem that must claim our attention is, however, the most pressing one, the problem of how to reform our outrageous divorce laws.

16

II

The Divorce Mess: A Solution

For both sexes in this society, caring deeply for anyone is becoming synonymous with losing.
—Herbert Hendin

Marriage and family are based on the need of the male to face his responsibility and to take his share in the process of reproduction and of the continuity of culture.
—Bronislaw Malinowski

DIVORCE AS IT operates in our society can, with a fair approximation to accuracy, be described as a robbery of the husband by the wife and her accessories in the legal profession, preceded by those formalities and perjuries deemed necessary to maintain the dignity of the law.

What would happen to our legislators if they were to permit husbands to do what they now permit wives to do: turn their spouses into the street; deprive them of their children, their homes, their furniture and appliances, their household pets, the good family car (though the wives would be permitted to retain the coupon book if there were still payments to be made on it); load them with debts, and compel them, under penalty of going to prison, to work and turn over as much as half or more of their income to their ex-husbands for the support of the children of whom they had been deprived?[1]

Legislators who perpetrated such a law would be torn to pieces by mobs of frenzied women. Yet the law just described is the existing law with the genders of the nouns and pronouns interchanged. It is a law that has generated disastrous effects extending far beyond injustice to individual men. It is destroying society by destroying the system of male motivation upon which all civilization rests.

As George Gilder has shown in his book *Sexual Suicide*, the difference between civilized and savage society is not found in the differing behavior of women, who are largely tied to maternal functions in both societies. It is found in the differing behavior of men. Civilized society channels male aggression and male energy into useful directions to do the work of society; savage society fails to do this, and male aggression and energy are expended in compulsive masculine rituals of war, hunting, gang fights, machismo, violence, and crime.[2]

Where are the high crime areas of our society—and where are there large numbers of families headed by women? The two questions have a single answer: matriarchy and violence are twins. The boys' vice-principal of your local high school, the man responsible for discipline, will tell you that the troublemakers are the boys from fatherless families and that the boys from motherless families are not a problem at all. Boys from fatherless homes frequently fail to learn what it means to be responsible and civilized men. They often grow up lacking self-respect, respect for authority, self-reliance, dignity, and magnanimity, incapable of doing the work of society. Girls from fatherless homes all too frequently produce fatherless families themselves, thus perpetuating matriarchy and violence into the next generation.

What motivates a man to do the work of society? Ask him and he will bring out his wallet and show you pictures of his family. The family is the great motivator of society; and this motivation has been greatly eroded in the last decade by feminism and has been destroyed for tens of millions of men by our divorce laws.

But there is a way of restoring this motivation and reforming these wretched laws which is so simple that the main problem in implementing it would be to persuade people that there could be such an easy solution to such an enormous evil. It would require nothing more than a stroke of the pen— and a little political courage. It is to abolish alimony and child-support payments in divorce cases. The idea is not so startling when one begins to consider it from the point of

18

view of men, of women, of children, and of society as a whole.

Men would benefit. In most cases—there would be many exceptions—the abolition of alimony and child-support would mean placing children in the custody of their fathers, who can best provide for them. These fathers would no longer be turned into the street, bewildered, shattered, and, save for the fear of prison, motiveless. They would be highly motivated men, more than ever essential providers for their children. Their role would indeed be augmented since they would be both breadwinners and housekeepers.

Women would benefit. Instead of being fretting parasites, using their children as hostages to ensure payments from men they hate,[3] they would be liberated from the household drudgery that is such a constant subject of complaint in feminist literature—liberated from "the great scourge" of marriage, as Mrs. Pankhurst called it. A mother encumbered with the custody of children cannot commit her full energies to a career in which she can hope to compete successfully with men who have supportive wives, or with childless and unencumbered women. She can be only half-committed to her job—usually a second-rate job—remaining dependent on child-support income given her by someone she probably detests, income that she knows will eventually cease when her children are grown, when she is older, when she is less marriageable, less competent to cope with a career. Without children—and with the children adding to the burdens of her ex-husband—she would be free to compete advantageously in the job market, devoting her full energies to her career, whereas her former husband would be burdened with a double role.

Women would acquire self-respect along with independence. And another group of women would benefit economically—the probable future stepmothers whom the husbands would need to care for their homes and children, and whom they could afford to marry and provide for if they were not burdened with the child-support and alimony payments that now commonly impoverish them.

Feminists say they wish to compete in a man's world. Surely the best way of facilitating such competition is to relieve them of the burden of their children, whose diaper-changing and nose-wiping is such a constant theme of

19

complaint with them. Mothers are at an economic advantage when they are thus disencumbered;⁴ fathers are no longer demoralized by the loss of their role; stepmothers are provided for; children grow up in the custody of the parent best able to provide for them. And both the mother and the stepmother have been offered the options the feminists aver that they should be offered—career and marriage. What could be more sensible, more just, more to the advantage of everyone—everyone except the lawyers and bureaucrats who profit from the destruction of families?

If custody were commonly given to fathers there would be no stigma attached to mothers not being given custody—this fear of stigmatization being a major motive with them now when courts almost automatically award children to mothers, and when, accordingly, their failure to do so creates a presumption of unfitness.

"The alimonized wife," writes the feminist Germaine Greer, "is no more free than she ever was." Even though most women would shrink from abandoning their children, she says, "this is precisely the case in which brutally clear rethinking must be undertaken." Both for her own and for her children's sake, she believes, a wife ought to "make a sensible decision" and let the husband have the children.

Children would benefit. There would be, for one thing, far fewer divorces. (In Los Angeles County, some 95 percent of divorces are filed by women.) And if divorce did occur, children would normally be better off in the father's custody, where they do not hold the status of meal tickets.

Women, according to the feminist psychologist Phyllis Chesler, are far more neurotic and unstable than men, more dependent on psychotherapy, more prone to depression, tantrums, nervous breakdowns, paranoia, and attempted suicide.⁵ The female sex, writes Freud, is "the sex certainly more predisposed to neurosis."⁶ "The principal instrument in the causation of neurosis in the child," say Ferdinand Lundberg and Marynia Farnham, "is the highly disturbed psychological organism, the mother."

Today, says Jean Curtin,

51 percent of mothers in the United States with preschool children work full time outside their

20

homes. . . . T. Berry Brazleton, who devotes more space in his books to "the working mother," always paints that mother as the most neglectful, neurotic and confused of them all. In his latest, *Toddlers and Parents,* he has his hypothetical mother sleeping late, rushing to get to work and feeding her baby an insufficient breakfast.

These horror stories have grave implications for the legion of nonworking mothers fearful of destroying the happiness of their children if they have to reenter the job market. Yet most women who work are doing so because they have to.[7]

They have to, that is, under the American system of divorce, which at present is destroying half of American marriages. But why, if the consequences of this system are so disastrous, do the courts, which are presumed to have the best interests of children at heart, so routinely give custody to mothers? The explanation is exceedingly simple: the courts are not interested in the best interests of children nearly as much as they are interested in the financial interests of the legal profession. The existing system is one that generates billions of dollars for this profession and that is the reason it has been inflicted upon us. A complementary reason is the amazing docility of the American male (alluded to in the preceding chapter). As Frederick Douglass said, what people are willing to put up with is what they will have to put up with.

Even the simple physical care of children might be better placed in the hands of fathers rather than mothers. According to R. F. Doyle, "Many stupid custody decisions result in tragedy. The number of child deaths and maimings by mother and boyfriends are appalling." According to the *Liberator* of September 1975,

> Betty Rollin, senior editor of the now defunct "Look" magazine, said, "The realities of motherhood can turn women into terrible people." Judging by 50,000 cases of child abuse yearly in the United States, this appears to be quite true.
>
> A Minnesota study of physical child abuse in

1967 showed the ratio of mother guilt to that of father guilt was 17 to 7. Professor Urie Bronfenbrenner, addressing a Congressional committee about child abuse, said, *"The most severe injuries occurred in single-parent homes, and were inflicted by the mother herself."* (Emphasis added.)

A mother's importance is greatest when children are quite young and her role decreases in importance with the passing years. Not so with the father's role. He must show his children how to become responsible adults, teach them the cardinal virtues of prudence, justice, temperance, and fortitude and the art of reasoning.[8] It is better for children to be in a family whose head becomes more essential with the passage of time rather than less. Children do not grow younger, they grow older, and while quite young ones, *at the time of the divorce*, might need their mothers more, there is reason to believe fathers should normally have custody. As Goldstein, Freud, and Solnit point out in their important book *Beyond the Best Interests of the Child*, it is of the utmost importance for a child to have *a continuity of relationship* with at least one caring adult. To change custody arrangements when the child becomes older—when he needs his mother less and his father more—is to break this continuity and to leave the child adrift emotionally and psychologically, not knowing where he can safely commit his loyalties and his growing ability to love. His emotional life is, consequently, likely to be superficial and suspicious, detached and withdrawn.

(The same is to be said about the currently fashionable proposal for joint custody, which would shuttle children from one parent to another and expect the children to be loyal alternately to one and then the other of two probably hostile people, or at least two people with different views on things that the child must necessarily become confused about.)

Society would benefit. The divorce rate would plummet. (In California, during the first nine months of 1977, there were more divorces than marriages!) The family, the roles of the sexes, and what George Gilder calls the sexual constitution of society would be reaffirmed. The subsidizing—and hence encouraging—of divorce would end. Wives would discover that marriage is an excellent arrangement for women—as indeed it is for men also. The admirable feminine virtues of patience and forbearance would be cultivated. Magnanimity would again become part of society's expectation for men. The scandalous absence of educational, cognitive, and verbal skills in our schoolchildren and college students—most visible among children from fatherless families—would at least be reduced.

The association between crime and matriarchy is obvious, though the feminists and welfare bureaucrats would prefer that the public didn't notice it, since patriarchal families would mean the demise of feminism and the erosion of the welfare empire. These people would much prefer that the public think crime is the result of poverty—and that, to eradicate it, taxpayers must dig deeper into their pockets for more money to finance Great Society and Head Start programs and larger AFDC payments, which, of course, have the added consequence of enlarging bureaucracies. If crime were caused by poverty, the American-Chinese, who have been up against heavy odds in our society for over a century, ought to have had one of the highest crime rates. They don't. They have the lowest crime rate—and they have patriarchal families. Much the same is true of the Japanese and the Jews— both groups with low crime and a patriarchal family structure. High crime and delinquency—and illegitimacy—come from those areas where there are enormous numbers of families headed by women—where Mom and the bureaucrats run things. The favelas of South American cities, impoverished beyond the imaginings of Watts and Harlem, barrios without paved streets, utilities, or underground sewage, where the inhabitants live in hovels improvised from packing crates and pieces of sheet metal, are not plagued by the kind of crime and violence found in American ghettos. It would seem to be a fair inference that the relative stability of these slums is related to the fact that they do not subsist on a system of government welfare which displaces fathers from their role as heads of families and sends them out to look for trouble.

Children living in families headed by fathers would be more properly socialized and civilized. There would be less of the absurdism and "mysterious acts of violence" of which Karl Bednarik has written—"outbursts of blind rage, incoherent criticism, aimless resentment, dreary grumbling . . .

23

apathetic, helpless, sulky resignation ... delinquency ... student riots . . . terrorism—often in response to seemingly arbitrary, accidental provocations."[9]

Most such acts are perpetrated by unmarried, sexually confused, and improperly socialized males—a fact recognized even by feminists, though they most illogically use it to "prove" the need for more feminism. The picture of these males drawn in such books as Karl Bednarik's *The Male in Crisis*, George Gilder's *Naked Nomads*, Alexander Mitscherlich's *Society Without the Father*, and Herbert Hendin's *Age of Sensation* is frightening—as is the picture of young women in the latter book. The destruction of the family in our society has made people afraid of intimacy, afraid of love. The commonest complaint made in campus health and counseling centers is sexual impotence, impotence accompanied by rage, which often can be controlled only by apathy.

No man can respect the system of law that gives him such a shabby deal as he receives in the divorce court—which requires him to actually *pay* a man, his wife's attorney, to help destroy his family, to deprive him of his children and his property,[10] and to attack his character, which permits three strangers, members of an odious profession, men with no interest in his welfare, to impose upon him an outrageously unjust arrangement depriving him of most of his motivations and laying heavy debts upon him for years, even for a lifetime—an arrangement often imposed without due process, the two lawyers and the judge retiring into chambers to facilitate the carving up of his family and his property, to prevent a record being kept that might permit later appeals, and—not incidentally—saving lawyers' time so that more cases may be processed and more fees generated.

Most of the charges made by the early feminists at Seneca Falls in 1848 could be made by men today. Try changing the gender of the italicized words in their 1848 document and see whether they do not apply to the situation of men now: "He has so framed the laws of divorce, as to what shall be proper causes, and, in case of separation, to whom the guardianship of the children shall be given as to be wholly regardless of the happiness of *women*—the law in all cases going upon a false supposition of the supremacy of *men*, and giving all power into *his* hands."

24

The divorce business has become so palpably dishonest that even the legal profession is embarrassed about it and accordingly is attempting to "reform" the scandal by perpetuating it under a new terminology. This is called "no fault" divorce. Divorce is renamed Dissolution of Marriage. Alimony is renamed Spousal Support. The Plaintiff is renamed the Petitioner. The Defendant is renamed the Respondent. And—and this is the real core of the reform—it is henceforth no longer necessary to prove the extreme cruelty of the husband to justify inflicting upon him a more grievous penalty than is imposed upon most low-income black felons. The necessary corollary to "no fault" is "no punishment"; but since that corollary would destroy the matriarchy and deprive the legal profession of billions of dollars, it must be avoided. Accordingly, the phony pretense that men were guilty of extreme cruelty was removed and replaced by the stipulation that they should be punished because they were innocent.

At the conclusion of Offenbach's comic opera *La Perichole* there occurs a delightful scene in which the Peruvian Viceroy, Don Andres, proclaims a general amnesty, releases all the prisoners from jail, gives them full pardon and allows them to return home. It is discovered, however, that there is an aged marquis who was imprisoned by mistake twelve years previously, and since he never committed a crime, he has done nothing for which he can be forgiven. He is accordingly sent back to prison.

Very funny. That's what's known in show business as a joke. Only *this* joke is not in an operetta. Under "no fault" divorce American fathers really do lose their children and their homes and income because they are male and because they are guilty of no fault.

Few divorced men can urge their sons to follow in their footsteps—to study hard, to work hard and be loyal to their employers, to marry and raise a family, to buy them a home and give them the good things of life. The sons know very well how society has rewarded their fathers for doing these things, and they do not look forward to marriages in which the same reward awaits them. Small wonder that homosexuality, machismo, violence, and alcoholism—those havens for battered and insecure males—are becoming endemic in our society, and indeed in every society where feminism has established itself.

Gerald Caplan, former director of the National Institute for Law Enforcement and Criminal Justice, tells us that "today, virtually no one—scholars, practitioners, and politicians alike—dares to advance a program which promises to reduce crime substantially in the near future. . . . We have more crime than any place in the world: more this year than last, and much, much more than we had in 1964."[11]

Something else that has increased—by more than a million in the last three years—is the number of families headed by women.[12] Fatherless families, those wallowing and teeming broodsows of the ills of society, generate far more delinquency and personality disorders than do normal or motherless families.[13] They are parasitic upon society and they generate millions of fellow parasites in the areas of welfare, social work, psychotherapy, law enforcement, and family law—all deriving their incomes from the destruction of the family.

The example of violence in the media has nothing to do with violence among the young. Japanese television, for example, is more violent than U.S. television and yet the Japanese crime rate keeps falling. According to Midori Suzuki of Forum for Children's Television, "There is no way to relate TV violence to crime in Japan because there is so little crime." When Professor Sumiko Iwao of the Keio University Institute for Communications Research in Tokyo was asked why so much protracted violence on Japanese TV failed to have the effect on Japanese children that it was thought to have on American children, she replied: "Mass media do not have the same impact in Japan. The family is still too strong, too influential in the lives and conduct of young people. In Japan, if a member of the family, even a juvenile, commits a crime, the act brings shame to all members of the family. This is a powerful deterrent to bad behavior."[14]

In the 1920s, in the Soviet Union, that country's leaders put into effect Engels's fatuous program for liberating women by destroying the family. The result was the same kind of crime, violence, and juvenile delinquency as we are witnessing in our own society, with this difference, however—that the Soviets acknowledged their error and reversed their policy,

26

and worked to strengthen the family rather than weaken it. "Soviet Russia today," wrote the sociologist Pitirim Sorokin in 1956, "has a more monogamic, stable, and Victorian family and marriage life than do most of the Western countries."[15]

The principal reason why we ought to abolish alimony and child-support payments is that it is right. No judge would, on the grounds that it would benefit a family's children, require a wife who lost custody of them to go to her ex-husband's home twice a week to vacuum his floors, wash his laundry, mop his kitchen, and prepare his family's meals. Yet male divorcées are routinely required to work two days or more a week for their ex-wives. That American males tolerate this outrage recalls (once again) Frederick Douglass's words, "What people are willing to put up with is what they will have to put up with."

The California lawmakers aver that a marriage may be dissolved "when the purposes of marriage are no longer served." But one of the main purposes of marriage is to provide economic security for women and children, and this purpose continues to be served under California divorce arrangements. The wife gets a divorce. The husband continues to perform his breadwinning functions. He gets a divorce only in the sense that he is relieved of his motivation for working.

Society, wrote James Freeman Clarke a century ago, is composed of families, as matter is composed of molecules and tissue is composed of cells. At a time when the problems of the world—hunger, overpopulation, ecology, energy, nuclear bombs, future shock—are converging towards what will evidently be the greatest crises and cataclysms of history, it is suicidal to do what our society is doing by its divorce laws—destroying its fundamental institution, the patriarchal family.

NOTES

1. "Regardless of the number of children or the unemployment of the wife, divorce courts tend to leave the husband with close to half of his net income," complains an anonymous, but evidently feminist, writer in an article entitled

"Justice for Women" in *Everybody's Money* (Summer 1978), p. 19.

2. What, the feminist will ask, of Margaret Mead's Tchambuli tribe, in which the women perform the managerial work and the men behave childishly and narcissistically? What of the Tchambuli, indeed? They are likewise engaging in compulsive rituals to prove their manhood, rituals at least as silly as machismo, gang-fighting, and motorcycling around in leather boots and leather jackets hung with iron crosses. It is true that in the case of this minute tribe, which was dying out when Mead observed it, the men were no great warriors. They *purchased* the prisoners whose brains they clubbed out to demonstrate their masculinity. See Gilder's remarks, *Sexual Suicide*, pp. 55ff.; Steven Goldberg, *The Inevitability of Patriarchy*, pp. 43ff.; and Arno Karlen, *Sexuality and Homosexuality*, p. 497.

3. "His erstwhile spouse, now socially saddled by her children, financially fettered, and facing a lonely and uncertain future, understandably feels sorely used and embittered. Should she reenter the dating rat-race, she perceives herself as dehumanized, fair game for philandering husbands and just another aging slab on a never-ending meat rack. Her antagonism toward her ex escalates, and the friendliest and most civil of divorces tend to sour. Some divorcées devote the remainder of their lives to a vendetta against their onetime loves, choosing vengeance over sanity, and often wreck both lives in the process. Previous comfortings are replaced by mutual cruelties, and the embattled participants become too preoccupied to understand." (Harvey Kaye, *Male Survival*, New York, Grosset and Dunlap, 1974, p. 136.)

4. "Divorced women have the lowest household incomes of any group of women surveyed. . . . One reason that divorced women are in the worst economic situation is that their income decreases markedly when their marriages end and they are able to save much less than single or married women. . . . Single women without children have a greater measure of economic freedom than the rest." (*Ms.* May 1978.)

5. According to Chesler (Introduction to *Women and Madness*, New York, Doubleday, 1972, p. vi):

"Chapter Four and the Appendix present an analysis of our

28

nation's 'mental illness' statistics from 1950 to 1969. These chapters document the extent to which women, more than men, and in greater numbers than their existence in the general population would predict, are involved in 'careers' as psychiatric patients: women who are having 'nervous breakdowns,' crying fits, temper tantrums, paranoid delusions; women who attempt suicide, who take unknown quantities of drugs to smother their anxieties, their hostilities, their ambitions, their panics, their sexual unhappiness—and their visions. In 1968 American women comprised 62% of the adult (ages eighteen to sixty-four) population in outpatient clinics, 61% of the adults in private hospitals—where they returned more frequently and were detained for longer periods than their male counterparts. Adult women currently compose two-thirds of the patients in Community Mental Centers and in private psychotherapeutic treatment. And most 'patients' over sixty-five, in asylums or in old-age homes, are, of course, women. (Our society does not overly like old age—or women.)"

6. *Dictionary of Psychoanalysis*, p. 168.

7. Brazleton is cited in *Family Circle*, October 1976.

8. According to Henry Biller, in *Father, Child and Sex Role* (Lexington, Mass., D.C. Heath and Co., 1971, p. 57,:

"Many investigators have found that the father-absent child often suffers from intellectual deficits. In a study involving Scottish children, Sutherland noted that those who were father-absent scored significantly lower on an intelligence test than did those who were father-present. Sutton-Smith, Rosenberg, and Landy found that males who became father-absent early in life were more likely to have lower college aptitude scores than were males whose fathers had not been absent.

"Maxwell administered the WISC to a large number of 8- to 13-year-old children referred to a British psychiatric clinic and reported that children whose fathers had been absent since the age of five performed below the norms for their age group on a number of sub-tests."

On p. 65:

"Hoffman reported data concerning the conscience development of 7th grade children. Father-absent boys consistently scored lower than father-present boys on a variety of moral indexes. They scored lower on measures of internal moral judgment, guilt following transgressions, acceptance of blame, moral values, and rule-conformity. In addition, they were rated as higher in aggression by their teachers which may also reflect difficulties in self-control."

On p. 57:

"Kohlberg . . . has reasoned that differences in the sex-role development of father-absent and father-present boys are related to the less mature cognitive functioning of the father-absent child. Kohlberg viewed the learning of socially defined concepts of sex-role as the primary ingredient of the sex-role development process and argued that many young father-absent boys lack certain types of cognitive experience, retarding both their intellectual and sex-role development."

On p. 59:

"Class grades and academic achievement test scores were examined, and it was found that the academic performance of the high father-present group was much superior to the other three groups. The early father-absent boys were generally underachievers, the late father-absent and low father-present boys usually functioned somewhat below grade level, but the high father-present group performed almost a year above grade level."

Other difficulties related to father-absence are discussed in Biller's *Paternal Deprivation* and Hans Sebald's *Momism: The Silent Disease of America*.

The increasing importance of fathers and decreasing importance of mothers is indicated by Nelson Foote: "It is the husband who usually outgrows the wife." (Cited in J. Bernard, *The Future of Marriage*, p. 44.)

9. Karl Bednarik, *The Male in Crisis*. New York, Alfred A. Knopf, 1970, p. 24.

10. Not all of it of course. "What have I gained for my client?" asks divorce lawyer Stuart Walzer, with impeccable reasonableness. "What have I gained for my client if we make a basket case out of her husband? She may not realize it in the midst of an angry divorce, but she is *depending* on his ability to continue earning money. If, however, her demands disable him, financially or psychologically, she'll find to her dismay that her husband is unable or unwilling to work. In turn, that

deprives her of the satisfaction she'd hoped to win." (Los Angeles Times, 3 August 1975.)

Those who suppose lawyers' fees in divorce cases are not excessive are those with modest incomes. The Society of Single Fathers newsletter of March 1977 tells of a case in which the lawyers pocketed over $50,000. I myself know of a wealthy man whose lawyers spun custody litigation out to $200,000.

11. "(C)rime has increased about 40% in the last ten years, and crimes against persons—violent crimes like mugging and rape . . . have reached epidemic proportions." (Human Events, 3 December 1977.)

12. As long ago as 16 July 1972 the Los Angeles Times ran the following story:

"March, 1971, census figures (the latest available) show that 6 million families with children under 18 are headed by women—about 12% of all American families. For years the figure stood constant at 10%, but the huge increase in divorces (715,000 in 1970) is making the fatherless family commonplace. . . . These women (family heads) are raising at least 20 million children. . . . (F)atherless families have been getting poorer and poorer, on the average. During the prosperous 1960s, the proportion of men and male-headed families in poverty dropped to an all time low of 6%, while the proportion of mother-child families in poverty went up to 36%."

13. According to Dr. Carlo Abruzzese (Santa Anna Star-Ledger, 20 October 1977):

"The consequences of parental deprivation are the most costly to society: 90% of children in trouble are from broken homes, according to Judge S. L. Vauvuris of the San Francisco Superior Court. . . . Juvenile delinquency, vandalism, mental disturbances, drug addiction, homosexuality and learning disabilities are just a few of the problems."

See also Chapter IV below and Tables 90ff. of Hathaway and Monachesi's Adolescent Personality and Behavior. Cf. the following from Biller, Father, Child and Sex Role, p. 39: "Bacon, Child, and Barry (Journal of Abnormal Psychology, 66:291ff.) discovered that societies with relatively low father availability have a higher rate of crime than do societies in which the father is relatively available."

14. *TV Guide*, 28 January 1978.

15. *The American Sexual Revolution*, Boston, Porter Sargent Publisher, 1956, p. 115:
"It is to be noted that, apart from the delinquency generated, it is *uneconomical* for the state to take over family functions—a fact which Marxists like to blur. Here is what the Marxist Caroline Lund says of the Soviet program of the 1920s:

> The Russian revolution, after taking the most radical steps ever taken by any country in laying the basis for the liberation of women, was unable to finish the job. A bureaucracy emerged which took steps backward. . . . The revolutionary Soviet government inherited this backwardness in attitudes. In addition, the extremely low level of technological development made it *impossible for the Soviet economy to fully assume the traditional economic responsibilities of the family*—care of the children and old people, food preparation, housing and clothing. *The family remained an economic necessity* as long as society did not have the resources to provide these alternatives to the mass of people. (*The Family: Revolutionary or Oppressive Force?*, p. 19; emphasis added.)

Simone de Beauvoir, who still clings to Engels's discredited theory (borrowed from Lewis Morgan) that woman was dethroned by the advent of private property and his notion that the state should take over most family functions, thus tries to avoid acknowledging the real—and notorious—reason for the failure of the Soviet program:

> It is difficult to make out through the haze of passionate and contradictory testimony just what woman's concrete situation really was (sc. in the 1920s); but what is sure is that today the requirements of repeopling the country have led to a different political view of the family: the family now appears as the elementary cell of society, and woman is both worker and housekeeper. Sexual

morality is of the strictest; the laws of 1936 and 1941 forbid abortion and almost suppress divorce; adultery is condemned by custom. Strictly subordinated to the State like all workers, strictly bound to the home, but having access to political life and to the dignity conferred by productive labor, the Russian woman is in a singular condition which would repay the close study that circumstances unfortunately prevent me from undertaking. (*The Second Sex*, New York, Alfred A. Knopf, 1953, p. 127.)

There is, of course, no mystery about why the Russians abandoned their experiment and returned to the family. Here is what Sorokin says of it:

Within a few years, hordes of wild, homeless children became a real menace to the Soviet Union itself. Millions of lives, especially of young girls, were wrecked; divorces skyrocketed, as also did abortions. The hatreds and conflicts among polygamous and polyandrous mates rapidly mounted—and so did psychoneuroses. Work in the nationalized factories slackened. (*American Sexual Revolution*, p. 114.)

As Olive Goldman says, "Mlle. de Beauvoir has been in some degree hoodwinked by propaganda regarding the alleged advantages enjoyed by women in Russia. Reliable reports from behind the Iron Curtain give ample proof that the equality of the sexes there is simply equality in slavery." (*SRL*, 21 February 1953.)

III

Custody for Men

At the first sign of any concerted effort on the
part of men to correct today's divorce mess,
women and divorce's profiteers are going to
rise en masse with emotional and self-
proclaimed righteous indignation. They have
to or they are likely to lose superabundant
benefits awarded by today's divorce meth-
ods. They will scream "motherhood." They
will protest in the name of "their" children's
welfare. They will revile men for not wanting
to do their duty—as they see it. Women and
divorce profiteers have a great deal to lose
through justice in our laws and courts. They
will not stand idly by and let men pluck this
rich plum from their tree of plenty.
—Charles Metz

There is no clear evidence of the value of the
mother-child tie as compared to the father-
child tie.
—Margaret Mead

MICHELET'S *Life of Martin Luther* records that when the great
reformer was first told about the discovery of Copernicus
that the apparent revolution of the heavens was illusory and
was actually produced by the rotation of the earth—"it being
the same with us as with men in a carriage or a ship, who
think they see the shore and the trees moving past them,"
—this was his reply:

So it is with the world nowadays; men, to be
thought clever, won't content themselves with
what others do and know. The fool wishes to
change the whole art of astronomy; but as holy
Scripture saith, Joshua commanded the sun, not
the earth, to stand still.[1]

34

In the fall of 1944, when Germany, in the face of inevitable defeat, accelerated the massacre of prisoners in its concentration camps to prevent their rescue by Allied armies, there appeared in the *New York Times Magazine* an article by Arthur Koestler entitled "On Disbelieving Atrocities." Koestler told of his desperate frustration in trying to persuade people that these massacres were really taking place. No one believed him. It was not the fashion to believe such things. Everyone remembered the fabricated atrocity stories of World War I.

Koestler would produce photographs smuggled from the camps at the risk of men's lives. He would relate stories, with circumstantial detail, of people known to himself who had been killed there. When an occasional look of comprehension seemed to dawn momentarily on his hearers' faces, he would think to himself, "Now you've got them. Hold them and make them know the truth." But the look would fade, to be replaced by one of polite skepticism and Koestler knew that he had failed once again.

What have such stories to do with the subject of the present chapter: Custody for Men? They illustrate the most important point of the chapter, "field direction." Field direction means going along with what everyone else thinks and does. Field direction is the reason why the idea of custody for fathers strikes most people as odd. The thing is not done—not nowadays. Everyone knows that children belong with their mothers.

And yet, a century ago, field direction worked the other way. The feminists at Seneca Falls made it one of their chief complaints that husbands were privileged to take children away from wives. When the strange notion that mothers might be given custody of children was proposed to John Stuart Mill he was sympathetic to the suggestion but declined to support it publicly since it was an idea "for which the human mind will not, for some time, be sufficiently prepared to make its discussion useful."[2]

In Japan, matters are not too different from what they were in England and America in Mill's day:

One "modan" (Japanese living in modern circles) Japanese now in America took into her own rooms

35

in Tokyo a pregnant young wife whose mother-in-law had forced her to leave her husband. Gradually she became interested in the baby she was soon to bear. But when the child was born, the mother came accompanied by her silent and submissive son to claim the baby. It belonged of course to the husband's family and the mother-in-law took it away. She disposed of it immediately to a foster home.[3]

The Hon. Mrs. Richard Norton, a nineteenth-century society hostess, left her husband when he removed their children to the home of a relative. She then found that—like millions of American males today—she had no rights of custody, or even access to them. And, again like millions of American males today, she had no rights to her own property.

Elizabeth Cady Stanton complained, in her *History of Women's Suffrage* (III, p. 290), that in the early nineteenth century a husband could take a wife's property and remove her children from her. According to the Corpus Juris Secundum, "at common law, and under some statutes, the primary right to the custody and care of minor children is generally in the father."[4]

In China, formerly, divorced men generally kept their children. And H. Ian Hogbin informs us that among the Melanesian Wogeo a wife will rarely initiate divorce proceedings, since the law will allow her husband to keep the children.[5]

There would be few divorces in America if our gavel-wielders had the common sense of the Melanesian Wogeo.

Hear now the most famous liberated woman in literature, Nora, in Ibsen's *A Doll's House*, written in 1878. Ibsen evidently never heard of the idea that wives—after liberating themselves—could take their children with them and use them as hostages:

> NORA: And I—how am I fitted to bring up the children?
> TORVALD: Nora!
> NORA: Didn't you say so yourself a little while ago—that you dare not trust me to bring them up?

36

TORVALD: In a moment of anger! Why do you pay any heed to that?

NORA: Indeed, you were perfectly right. I am not fit for the task. There is another task I must undertake first, I must try and educate myself—you are not the man to help me in that. I must do that for myself. And that is why I am going to leave you now.

TORVALD: (springing up) What do you say?

NORA: *I must stand quite alone,* if I am to understand myself and everything about me. It is for that reason that I cannot remain with you any longer.

TORVALD: To desert your home, your husband and your children! And you don't consider what people will say!

NORA: I cannot consider that at all. I only know that it is necessary for me.

TORVALD: It's shocking. This is how you would neglect your most sacred duties.

NORA: What do you consider my most sacred duties?

TORVALD: Do I need to tell you that? Are they not your duties to your husband and your children?

NORA: I have other duties just as sacred.

TORVALD: That you have not. What duties could those be?

NORA: Duties to myself.

TORVALD: Before all else, you are a wife and a mother.

NORA: I don't believe that any longer. I believe that before all else I am a reasonable human being, just as you are—or at all events, that I must try and become one. I know quite well, Torvald, that most people would think you right, and that views of that kind are to be found in books, but I can no longer content myself with what most people say, or with what is found in books. I must think things for myself and get to understand them. . . . (puts the shawl around her) Goodbye, Torvald. *I won't see the little ones. I know they are in better hands than*

mine. As I am now, I can be of no use to them. . . .
Listen, Torvald. *I have heard that when a wife
deserts her husband's house, as I am doing now,
he is legally freed from all obligations toward her.*
In any case, *I set you free from all your obligations.
You are not to feel yourself bound in the slightest
way,* any more than I shall. *There must be perfect
freedom on both sides.* See, here is your ring back.
Give me mine. . . . Now it is all over. I have put the
keys here. The maids know all about everything in
the house—better than I do. Tomorrow, after I have
left her, Christine will come here and *pack my own
things that I brought with me from home.* I will
have them sent after me. . . .
   TORVALD: Let me help you if you are in want.
   NORA: *No, I can receive nothing from a stranger.*
                                    (Emphasis added.)

   She will leave her husband's home and return to her
father's home, in order that she may be independent of a man,
and she will send her maid to pick up her things—truly the
prototype of the feminists of our own day, who emancipate
themselves from dependence upon husbands by becoming
dependent upon ex-husbands or who clamor for subsidies
from Big Brother on the grounds that they are lesbians or
unmarried and have no ex-husbands to support them—and
who indeed claim indemnification for past discrimination by
a society which failed to understand that it needed lesbians
and unmarried women as much as it needed wives and
mothers. Despite the apparent reversals, the nature of the
underlying dependencies remains the same. And of course
Big Brother has to tax males if he is to rescue the divorced
princesses and pay his own salary. If Ibsen were writing
today he would have left the doll's house in the possession of
the doll.

   The plain fact is (we are informed by a divorcée
   named Jeanne Cambrai) that being divorced is fun.
   . . . Divorceés are the romantics of life. They would
   still be married if they were not. . . . For the first

time in your life you're in control of your own
destiny.[6]

Translation: You are relieved of the responsibilities of marriage and you can be sassy to the ex-husband who supports
you and who formerly had a say in how the money he earned
was to be spent. Now he, who once made decisions, is compelled to submit to your own decisions where family matters
are concerned. Lucky you, who have the lawyers on your side.
Less lucky, perhaps, is your daughter, who finds herself surrounded by bewildered and impotent young men who don't
seem to know quite what a man's role in this society is supposed to be. Very much less lucky is your son who, if he is
unwise enough to get married, must wonder what the future
holds for him in addition to paying alimony and child support
money to a tart.

"When you are divorced, you like what you see," Cambrai
exults. "You open your eyes to a world that is in technicolor
and a good place to be alive in, and like a child you want to get
at it right away." "It's a good feeling." "For those of you who
are still hanging in there," she sneers, "don't feel smug and
virtuous."

> It is disgusting to think so little of yourself that
> you can accept a lifestyle that is not fulfilling to
> you as a human being.

(It is not, however, disgusting to accept the child-support
money that puts you in charge of your destiny.)

> In fact, the best place for long-suffering married
> persons is in the trash can. Their contribution to
> life is nil. It may seem a bit strong to hear yourself
> called human refuse, but what else do you call a
> person who is so screwed up that she would waste
> her whole life rather than stand on her own feet?

And she adds this theological reflection:

> You could get to heaven, of course, but what if God

says, "Sorry, love, you missed the point of being on earth. You were supposed to have a good time!"

"Married *men*," she informs us, "have a terrific time."

I would love all men to have a terrific time naturally because one special man is what I want in my life and I want him to be happy. But if his happiness depends on my playing doormat, well he can have a terrific time with someone else. Divorcées can have that kind of self-respect.

"Let him go!" she crows. "Throw him out. . . . Take the kids too, if you want, but get away from HIM."
    Good to know she wants all men to be happy. If she had not said so, a reader might have supposed she was enjoying her triumph over her former husband who, even though she (naturally) wishes him to be happy, is a "rat" who refused to discuss divorce arrangements "sanely." She tells how with the aid of a lawyer[7] her vision expanded to see the world in technicolor, to experience the good feelings of life, to become a romantic, and to stand on her own feet:

When I first wanted a divorce, what I *wanted* was $100 a month for each of the children (there were three), the freedom to take them with me if I traveled, and their medical bills paid. . . . But what I did get was $75 per month per child, $200 a month for me for one year, a house I didn't want,[8] the kids' medical bills paid, and an order restricting their movements to the state.

Thus it is that women become "independent" of men and lead lives of romance. Thus it is that lawyers generate fees "regardless of the cost"—to the husbands, that is. "Divorce," Roberta Greene informs us, "can be an indication of maturity. Even the process of getting a divorce can be a maturing experience. Consider the settlement proposals as your Bill of Rights, and assert yourself as a deserving human being.[9] You have nothing to lose but a husband you don't want anyway.[10] Independence as a mature woman is a wonderful experience."[11] "Above all," she says, "if there are children involved, and you are assuming custody, remember that you are probably going to be negotiating for them, since you are maintaining that house, car, dog and assorted fish for their benefit. They have a right to be raised in the style to which they are accustomed if the marriage had been maintained." The man, in other words, has no such right—only the obligation to be docile.

The title of Cambrai's book is *Once Is Enough*, and it is a well-chosen title if it refers to the woman's privilege of shackling a man financially by committing matrimony with him. Lawyers and feminists are fast-draw specialists. According to the attorney Amy Fixler, a conscientious lawyer can only advise the wives to file for divorce at the first inkling of marital trouble: "You just can't tell a woman to hang in there, hoping for a reconciliation."[12] No, indeed; not if you are a lawyer who hopes to collect a fee from her husband.

"Should you ask for alimony?" asks Susan Ross in her book *The Rights of Women*.[13] Her answer reveals the typical feminist mentality, with its incomprehension of the nature of the sexual constitution of society and its view of men as mere objects of prey to be hunted down with the aid of lawyers:

> Probably, if you are in the situation of most wives. Many women have begun to feel guilty about asking for alimony—perhaps in response to those men who are clamoring that alimony is "anti" women's liberation and oppresses men. The fact that these same men have not taken up any other banner of women's liberation provides a definite clue to their real motives. They want to get out of their marriages with as much money as possible, while absolving themselves of responsibility for the financial situation of their wives.

She means *ex*-wives. Husbands are willing to accept financial responsibility for *wives*. The pretense that only husbands, and not wives, "want to get out of their marriage with as much money as possible" requires no comment.

41

Whether men want to admit it or not, marriage [translation: *divorce*] still places women at a tremendous disadvantage. . . . Society encourages them to get married, to bear and rear children. [It formerly also encouraged them, as feminists and lawyers do not, to *stay* married and let their husbands provide for them.] This further decreases a woman's wage-earning capacity; for even when she has somehow managed to acquire education or training, she loses work experience and her own self-confidence during the years of child-rearing. [The fact that the husband provides for his family during the child-rearing years is thus translated from a benefit into a grievance.] Many women work to put their husbands through medical school or other kinds of extended education without ever receiving comparable training themselves, or even a repayment of the money. [Translation: Many women have the sense to realize that it is easier to acquire a doctor's income by marrying a doctor than by studying for seven years and passing stiff examinations.]

Nor [she continues] are women paid for their years of work in the home even though this work has real economic value. [Translation: Most of the family's paycheck is spent by the wife, but since it is made out in the husband's name, the wife is not "paid."] Thus they have no way to acquire property unless the husband "gives" it to them. [Here we see the quintessential grasping greediness of the feminist—her materialism. Joint and community properties aren't really *hers,* since someone else shares in their possession. She wants to have them all to herself, to be alone in her countinghouse, fingering her coins, fondling and caressing her bullion and her ingots.]

Finally, she makes a legitimate complaint:

Society also encourages most women to take custody of the children upon divorce—again without compensation.

42

It is the argument of this chapter and of other parts of the present book that this policy is a mistake: in most cases of divorce, children should probably be placed in the custody of the father. She goes on to speak of the "financial disabilities aggravated, or caused, by marriage," as though a husband's support of his family during marriage were no benefit whatever. The disabilities include:

> unequal educational opportunities [translation: greater demands made upon the husband], unequal employment opportunities [translation: more arduous work by the husband], and an unequal division of family responsibilities, with no compensation for the spouse who works in the home [translation: the husband works harder, dies eight years younger, and the wife spends three-quarters of the family's paycheck].

She suggests that husbands may try to place the blame for this "discrimination" on society, and is half-tempted to agree:

> The husband, however, benefits from *the system's discrimination in his favor* [it would be difficult to explain this discrimination to a man who had lost his children and his home], and there is no valid reason to allow him to carry away the fruits of an unfair bias. Moreover, the husband is often responsible for any unequal division of housekeeping responsibilities and lack of pay for the "housekeeper." [A possibility deserving serious consideration: *accede* to the demand for "wages for housewives"—and charge them rent and make them buy their own food and clothing.] After all, husbands acquiesce in the societal demand that the wife stay home [translation: husbands agree to provide for their wives] and it is a rare man indeed who would even consider staying home himself with the children so the wife could advance her career. [Translation: It is a rare wife indeed who is as highly motivated, or would work as hard and

earn as much money, as her husband. And it is a rare wife who doesn't know her husband works harder and will die younger than she.] If the husband would help rear the children, he and his wife could come much closer to equalizing their wage-earning capacities.

There is a profound misconception here. Equalizing wage-earning capacities is no purpose of marriage. The purpose of marriage, as Bronislaw Malinowski has well said, is to get *men* to cooperate in the process of creating families and rearing children. It is this that makes *neoteny* possible—the prolongation of childhood, so that children may remain open, receptive, exploratory, secure, playful—and helpless—for a prolonged period, so that they may grow slowly and securely and become integrated socially into the species that constitutes the greatest success story to be found among the two billion animal species that have inhabited the terraqueous globe—and the only species in which the male plays a role fully comparable in importance to that of the female in the rearing of children.

His role is to protect and provide for a family. No viable society (though there have been some decaying and very primitive ones) has ever found a meaningful role for its males other than this; and it is the feminist attempt to deprive men of their "need . . . to face their responsibility to take their share in the process of reproduction and of the continuity of the culture" which is eroding the sexual constitution of our society. The results, if they succeed in their program of making women "independent" of men, might be describable as ghettos without AFDC. When Ms. Ross writes of equalizing the wage-earning capacities of wives and husbands, this is what she is aiming at—though of course she has no understanding of this fact. "Paternity," writes George Gilder,

as a cultural invention, will not serve to give the man a durable role in the family; and there is virtually no society that successfully relies on it to keep the man actively present. To keep the man present and to preserve the nuclear family as the prevailing institution, even love will not long suffice. He must be needed in a practical and material way. . . .

Whether the society can socialize most of its males—integrate them into both the community and the ecomomy—will determine its tranquility and growth. It will decide whether government has to spend much of its time and energy in controlling men or whether the men will willingly contribute their labor and spirit to the larger society.[14]

Ms. Ross thinks it a matter of regret that most men don't wish to do half the housework while they let their wives earn half the income. "When married, they expect their wives to assume most of the responsibility for rearing the children"—which is to say, when married they expect to support their families. "When divorced, many of them expect their wives to take custody of the children." They expect it with good reason, since their lawyers assure them they have no chance of gaining custody themselves and since they know that judges lack the courage to keep their oath of office requiring them to administer impartial justice—in other words, to break with a tradition that is extremely lucrative to the legal profession. "Their wives," Ms. Ross thinks, "ought to be compensated for the extra work the men are avoiding" when they become divorced. Her words must have a peculiarly and insolently ironic sound to a man who is supporting two households. The sincerity of her argument might be tested by posing the following question: If a father were given custody of his children in a divorce case, ought the ex-wife to contribute to his support? Of course not: here men and feminists are in full agreement. The solution for the alimony/child-support extortion system is not to have a few token males receive payments from ex-wives, but to abolish alimony and child-support payments altogether, when, in the language of the California legislators, "the purposes of marriage are no longer served."

"Alimony," writes R. F. Doyle,

is a carryover from an obsolete type of limited divorce, *a mensa et thoro*, wherein the husband was still liable for the wife's support; an early form of

45

separate maintenance. It wasn't applicable to absolute divorce, *a vinculo matrimonii*; but it is so in modern times. Its purpose before emancipation was to support destitute, incapacitated ex-wives. Now it has been corrupted into the notion that an ex-wife has a right (in the words of one judge) "to continue to live in the manner to which she has become accustomed. . . . " (Powers vs. Powers; Mo. Ct App, St. Louis Dist, 9/16/75; 1 FLR 2795) [15]

Ms. Ross believes that even the cadavers of ex-husbands should be made to pay:

> You should make special arrangements for the life insurance to insure that there will be a viable policy to cover alimony and child support if your husband should die. One arrangement is for your husband to give you the incidents of ownership on the policy, so that he cannot use the policy as security for a loan or change the named beneficiaries. Another approach is to request alimony money to make the premium payments yourself; this insures that your husband will not let the insurance policy lapse.[16]

And the grasping, flat-faced insolence goes on:

> Work and education-related expenses should also be emphasized because they are the kinds of expenses most lawyers tend to overlook for a woman. Both are important for your own well-being, too, because being busy will make it easier to adjust to the change and because the vast majority of women will never receive enough alimony to live on comfortably.

This system of squeezing the male for everything he can be taken for is incontestably one of the reasons why so many young men are turning from marriage to shacking-up arrangements with their girl friends or to homosexuality. It is

46

one reason why millions of young women entering their reproductive years will never have a normal family life, but will instead become feminists, lesbians, and parasites upon society. It is a reason why—particularly now that it has become fashionable among actresses—many of them will bring bastards into the world who will themselves, in disproportionate numbers, become parasites or predators upon society. Such considerations would never occur to Ms. Ross, obsessed as she is with sweating the last farthing out of husbands and ex-husbands. Nor would she consider the fact that most women simply cannot compete with most men on the job market because they lack the male motivation for doing so. A woman privileged to be provided for lacks motivation for work and is uncompetitive with a man who knows that he *must* provide.

Ms. Ross's program is obviously one for generating fatherless families, the subject of the next chapter. One cannot help thinking of George Kennan's theory that the enormous number of fatherless families created in Germany by the slaughter of World War I was a principal cause of the rise of Naziism, a system satisfying the fatherless child's pathetic search for a father-surrogate with whom he could find himself in sympathetic resonance. Hitler hated his father intensely. Many other charismatic paranoids such as Charles Manson, Daniel DeFreeze, and Andreas Baader came from fatherless families. More about this in Chapter IV.

"There is no one correct answer," says Ms. Ross, to the question of how much alimony, child support, and property a woman's lawyer should get for her.

> At present, one third to one half of the property, plus one third to one half of the husband's *net* income as *gross* alimony and child support is considered the upper limit. Women ought to debate whether this is in fact a good standard.

Men ought to debate this too. Men ought to debate whether a fairer arrangement would not be *no* alimony, *no* child support and a strict fifty-fifty division of the *community* property.[17]

Ross goes on:

> Those who strongly view marriage as a partner-
> ship, in which each partner does work that is
> equally valuable, might like to see women get one
> half of all property [n.b., she does not say com-
> munity property] and enough alimony to leave each
> party with equal cash on hand after both deduct
> certain fixed expenses such as money used solely
> for the children (child support) and taxes. That is,
> wife and husband will have equal net incomes after
> the divorce.
>
> Other women might prefer to examine the eco-
> nomic situation more closely.

The economic situation should indeed be examined more
closely. Ross's proposal is that wives shall take husbands'
children, homes, and property, while permitting them to keep
the family debts; that the husbands, after paying their own
expenses and child support money to the ex-wives, shall
then split what they have left fifty-fifty for the purpose of allowing these ex-wives a fair alimony. And her second para-
graph goes on to suggest that this is perhaps not quite a good
enough split from the woman's point of view.

One stands in exophthalmic astonishment at such effron-
tery. "Those who strongly view marriage as a partnership"
are evidently presumed to view divorce as a master-
bondslave relationship in which the woman's withdrawal of
her services from the partnership is to be compensated by
the increased contribution of the husband.

"Prostitutes don't sell their bodies," the radical feminist
Flo Kennedy informs us, "they rent their bodies. Housewives
sell their bodies when they get married—they cannot take
them back—and most courts do not regard the taking of
woman's body by her husband against her will as rape."[18]

Very well. One might have hoped that marriage was a
familial relationship based on love rather than on merely
commercial considerations. But in any event renting and selling are legitimate and honorable commercial transactions in
which each party exchanges something of value for something he wants. What, then, is the proper name for a transac-

tion between an ex-wife and an ex-husband, a transaction in which the former uses coercion to compel the latter to yield his property to her—and in return performs no reciprocal services whatever? The name for this transaction is robbery. Feminists are almost unanimous in denouncing marriage on the grounds that it makes women financially dependent upon men. Why, then, do they not denounce alimony and child-support payments which equally make women dependent upon men? Obviously, their real objection is not to the dependency but to the performing of reciprocal services. In any case, they should be taken at their word: the degrading business of making ex-wives dependent upon ex-husbands should be ended. Nor must men permit things to evolve as they have in Scandinavia, where, the feminists assure us, society is ten years ahead of America. According to Neil Elliott,

> The late Dr. Kirsten Auken, the "Danish Kinsey," reported that in about 60 percent of all cases it has been the Scandinavian mother's specific wish to have a baby out of wedlock. Very often she has selected the male only for his stud qualities and afterward wants nothing to do with him: "No, I don't want to marry him. He's a jerk. I never even liked him."[19]

Scandinavia is becoming—as America is becoming—a society of tarts, parasites, bureaucrats, and taxpayers—and the taxpayers, the only ones with any motive for cleaning up the mess, seem to imagine this is the most natural arrangement in the world. "The highest increases in illegitimacy in recent years," wrote Neil Elliott in 1970, "have taken place among teenage girls—particularly the fifteen- to nineteen-year-old group—where illegitimacy has tripled since 1939, doubled since 1950."[20] Illegitimacy in Iceland is 30 percent. When the feminists tell us about the liberation of women, this is what they mean. Of course, they *do* need men to pay the taxes to pay the bureaucrats to pay the tarts to take care of their bastards.

The case for alimony and child support rests upon two

assumptions. Assumption number one is that women are the equals of men. Assumption number two is that women are inferior to men. Both assumptions are needed. If only the first is made, then the conclusion would follow that women do not need to be subsidized by men. But they must be subsidized if they are to be made equal. Ergo—alimony and child-support payments.

The quotation from Ross given earlier continues as follows:

> This view (i.e., of marriage—and therefore divorce—as a partnership) would use property settlement and alimony to compensate women [=perpetuate for women] only for financial damages [=advantages] incurred [=acquired] through marriage. Women who have stayed home for years rearing the family and doing elaborate housework would charge damages for each year of loss of wages, loss of associated fringe benefits (paid vacations, sick leave, medical-insurance coverage, pension plans), and decrease in wage-earning capacity, plus any continued loss of these items after the divorce.

A society which could persuade its females that the institution of marriage was thus disadvantageous to them must expect to persuade its males that the twin institution of marriage-cum-divorce has nothing to offer *them*—no inducements towards living responsibly and making long-term commitments. Benjamin Franklin well said, "A single man has not nearly the value he would have in a state of union. He is an incomplete animal. He resembles the odd half of a pair of scissors." But the "state of union" of which he speaks no longer exists. A single man may be an incomplete animal, but his condition is Arcadian bliss compared to the condition of a divorced man who has been deprived of his children and driven out of his home. What John Stuart Mill wrote of wives a century ago is precisely applicable to ex-husbands today:

> The law of servitude in marriage is a monstrous contradiction to all the principles of the modern

world, and to all the experience through which those principles have been slowly and painfully worked out. It is the sole case, now that negro slavery has been abolished, in which a human being in the plenitude of every faculty is delivered up to the tender mercies of another human being. . . . Marriage is the only actual bondage known to our law. There remain no legal slaves, except the mistress of every house.[21]

Betty Roszak quotes Robert Briffault as declaring "Woman is to man a sexual prey; man is to woman an economic prey," and comments on his assertion as follows:

This kind of oppression (i.e., of women) cuts across all economic class lines, even though there may be social differences between streetwalker Jane X, housewife Joan Y, and debutante Jacqueline Z. One may sell her body for a few dollars to the likeliest passerby; one for a four-bedroomed house in the suburbs; and one for rubies and yachts. But all must sell their bodies in order to participate in the bargain. Yet if women were to refuse to enter into the sexual bargain, they not only would refute the masculine idea of women as property,[22] but they also would make it possible to free men from the equally self-destructive role of sole breadwinner. Thus there would be a chance to break the predatory cycle.[23]

Normal men and women don't want to break the cycle. The cycle is what holds society together. The man works at what is usually a dull job in order that he may be exploited—as a provider for his family. This role is not destructive, as the greater longevity of married men proves. If feminists wish, as they profess to wish, to free men from a destructive role, they could begin by emancipating men from the payment of alimony and child support. The well-known fact that normal women delight in being sex-objects requires no comment; this role is the last thing they wish to be liberated from.

What feminist talk about liberating men really signifies is

their desire to possess the advantages of being men without assuming the disadvantages. They want fifty-one senatorships and in return offer men the privilege of crying, whiffling, and having hysterics.

None of the hypocrisies of the legal profession is as frequently and sanctimoniously expressed as its concern for the best interests of children. The following case, cited from the *Family Law Reporter,* is one of many showing the bench's lack of any such concern:

> The Kings County New York Supreme Court is still a court that adheres to this old doctrine and by applying the "tender years presumption" defeats a divorced father's effort to retain custody of his son—of whom he has had custody since parting from his spouse well over two years ago. (L. vs. L, 6/17/76).
>
> The former wife had been thrown out of her parents' home shortly after the couple had separated. Without either financial resources or employment, the wife, the court finds, had turned to the father of their nine-month-old son for temporary care of the child since she was without means to care for herself or the baby at the time. That the now-remarried father has been quite successful in rearing his son is noted by the court. However, permanent custody is still unavailable to the father despite his love and attention. Only under the most unusual circumstances, the court declares, would any leeway be found to afford an equally fit natural father custody of a young child.[24]

The devastating nature of such a decision is hard for adults to comprehend, since the adult time sense is so different from that of a young child and since adults seldom understand the urgency of a child's need to relate lovingly to a caring adult. Goldstein, Freud, and Solnit speak well of the need of every child for *unbroken continuity* of affectionate and stimulating relationships with an adult, and they call into question "those custody decisions which split a child's placement between two parents or which provide the noncustodial parent with the right to visit or to force the child to visit. Such official invitations to erratic changes and discontinuity in the life of a child are but illustrative of many determinations in law which run contrary to the often-professed purpose of the decisions themselves—to serve the best interests of the child.[25] The crucially important argument of these writers deserves to be quoted at length:

> Placement . . . must be treated as the emergency that it is for the child. . . . Three months may not be a long time for an adult decisionmaker. For a young child it may be forever. . . . Emotionally and intellectually an infant and toddler cannot stretch his waiting more than a few days without feeling overwhelmed by the absence of parents. . . . The child feels suddenly deserted by all the known persons in his world to whom he has learned to attach importance. His new ability to love finds itself deprived of the accustomed objects and his greed for affection remains unsatisfied. His longing for his mother [in the present case, his father] becomes intolerable and throws him into states of despair which are very similar to the despair and distress shown by babies who are hungry and whose food does not appear at the accustomed time. For several hours or even for a day or two this psychological craving of the child, the "hunger" for his mother [in this case, father] may override all bodily sensations. There are some children of this age who will refuse to eat or to sleep. Very many of them will refuse to be handled or comforted by strangers. . . . Observers seldom appreciate the depth and seriousness of this grief of a small child. Their judgment of it is misled for one main reason. This childish grief is short-lived. Mourning of equal intensity in an adult person would have to run its course throughout a year; the same process in the child between one and two years will normally be over in 36 to 48 hours. It is a psychological

error to conclude from this short duration that the reaction is only a superficial one and can be treated lightly.[26]

The father in this case was both the biological and the "psychological parent." The mother was, from the child's point of view, a complete stranger; and in placing the child in her custody the court inflicted a serious injury on it. Such injury goes beyond the child itself and the father. To other children in the family, say Goldstein, Freud, and Solnit, "the knowledge that the state can take the new child away is experienced as a threat. . . . [T]he detrimental impact on the health and well-being of the child who is already a member of the family is incalculable."[27]

Invoking the "best interests of the child" means, in effect, custody for mothers, fees for lawyers, and salaries for social workers, psychiatrists, and so forth. It is time to inquire whether this really does serve the best interests of the child. A great deal of research indicates that it does not. Much of this research has been consolidated and marshaled by Charles Metz in his important book *Divorce and Custody for Men,* to which the following paragraphs are heavily indebted.

Investigators from organizations such as the National Institute of Mental Health, the Institute of Developmental Studies of the New York Medical College, the Walter Reed Child Psychiatry Clinic, and many major universities have suggested that much of the psychological disturbance of children stems from mothers. Montgomery County, Maryland, one of the wealthier and better-educated areas in the country, has traced about a third of its juvenile crime to single-parent homes headed by women, and the predominant part of the rest to homes from which the father was frequently absent. Investigators such as Dr. Loren Mosher of the NIMH, Dr. Walter Mischel, and others have found from cross-cultural studies they conducted that poverty is not as important a factor in juvenile crime as the absence of a competent and loving father. Other relevant findings are thus summarized by Metz:

(1) Children with a father in the house generally have higher ratings on intelligence tests than

children living in homes without a father.

(2) Competent and loving fathers contribute materially to the mental health of children and are capable of serving as an effective buffer between a son and a domineering mother.

(3) Fathers are important in providing a masculine image for their sons. Fathers are important in developing femininity in their daughters.[28]

Under existing divorce arrangements, which automatically award children to mothers, there will inevitably be large numbers of women who want custody for the wrong reasons—to ensure child support or welfare payments or occupation of the family residence, to enjoy triumphing over ex-husbands, or to use children as status symbols to demonstrate that the court deems them to be fit mothers, something that would be in question if fathers got custody. These reasons would not apply in cases where fathers retained their children, when the presumption would be virtually certain that their concern really was the best interests of the children.

A constant theme of complaint in feminist literature is the misery of wives. Jesse Bernard's *The Future of Marriage* is often cited by feminists to prove this (though to be sure the tables in her own Appendix disprove it: 93 percent of married women describing themselves as either "very happy" or "pretty happy"). Bernard complains of "woman's extra load of economic dependency added to the emotional dependency" as being the worst part of her lot. In other words, the poor things have their bills paid for them by cruel husbands. The solution to this problem is the same as the solution of the woman's other principal burden, the drudgery of child rearing: return her to her former state of single blessedness by taking her children from her and removing the burden of her dependency upon her husband or ex-husband.

Custody for fathers would greatly reduce the number of divorces as well as the congestion in our courts, this being a major reason urged by the legal profession for increased subsidization of itself by the taxpayer. Indeed, merely getting rid of the quaint custom of forcing husbands to subsidize the destruction of their own families by paying their wives' lawyers' fees would have a beneficial and stabilizing effect on the structure of families, in addition to removing a part of the burden of dependency from wives.

A female lawyer named Aleta Wallach cites the Carnegie Commission's *Opportunities for Women in Higher Education* as saying "probably the most important factor tending to discriminate against women in admission to graduate study is a variety of rules and informal policies discouraging admission of students who wish to study on a part-time basis." And she goes on to comment, "A lack of part-time study programs for women who have child-care and domestic responsibilities is a major barrier to women's entrance into law and other professional schools. Obviously such women compete at a disadvantage with men students whose wives or girlfriends either support them financially or care for their households and children."[29] It sounds as though she would like to legislate that a part-time student must not be disadvantaged vis-à-vis a full-time one, and that it must not be advantageous to a man to be married—aims that would be difficult to achieve. Why not instead permit the woman to be a full-time student while hobbling the man with the child-care responsibilities? She could then not merely compete with him, but compete advantageously.

Ross Parks, a University of Illinois psychologist, declared following a five-year study that fathers are just as good at caring for infants as mothers. Parks claims to have disproved "the four myths of fatherhood"—that fathers are uninterested, are less nurturing, tend to assume noncaretaking roles, and are less competent. He believes that the importance of feeding has been narrowly regarded as the exclusive province of mothers. In any case, every parental function other than breast feeding has been shown by study after study to be as well performed by fathers as by mothers.[30]

According to Gloria Steinem, the American child's problem is too much mother and too little father; but her solution to this problem is less of both. To make it possible for both parents to work, there should be free nurseries and school lunches, service companies to handle all the household chores, housing complexes with built-in cafeterias for the entire family, the assumption of more responsibility by the whole community for the children.

Steinem, like her fellow feminists, thinks there are no "natural" sex roles. She agrees with former Prime Minister Olof Palme who, in a speech delivered in Washington in the spring of 1978, said that in Sweden it is *human beings* who will be emancipated, and that any politician who declared that the woman ought to have a different role from the man's would be regarded as something from the Stone Age. It would be interesting to hear the former Prime Minister (and Steinem) explain the non-Stone Age character of the following passage from Birgitta Linner's *Sex and Society in Sweden:*

> Following finalization of the divorce, the *wife's* allotted alimony will depend on *her needs* as compared with *her husband's ability to pay. It can happen* that the woman *may* be obliged to support the man. *Generally,* a claim for alimony *must have some justification.* A divorcée in good health and capable of earning her own living will *seldom* get alimony *indefinitely.* If, on the other hand, she has not worked for several decades or is over fifty and *accustomed to a high standard of living,* the court may rule that *the husband owes her a reasonable sum despite her potential earning capacity.* If the *wife* has custody of the children, *naturally* the husband must contribute to their support, and vice versa.[31]

One more feminist quote, this from Kate Millett, urging that there is nothing "natural" about sex roles:

> It is also to be expected that, even though it is intellectually understood that (beyond breast feeding) the assignment of child care is cultural rather than biological, middle class Americans will let that slip by and infer that child birth must mean child care, the two together again constitut-

ing "biology." It is one of conservatism's favorite myths that every woman is a mother.[32]

A myth no doubt. But a myth that provides the rationale for awarding custody to ex-wives and fiscal amercements to ex-husbands—a myth that enables bureaucracies to step into families as father substitutes. But try turning Ms. Millett's argument around: if the assignment of child care is cultural rather than "natural" or "biological," is this not a reason why society ought to *teach* girls to accept this assignment? If it were biological, it would not need to be taught. If boys and girls are taught that being a housewife and mother is feminine and not expected of boys, then the sexes are steered away from competing with each other. If girls are taught that they should compete with boys in football and chess, society will produce some moderately good female football and chess players—none outstanding—and legions of frustrated women who will regard themselves as failures in areas where they have been told they are expected to succeed.

The point requiring emphasis in the present connection is not that women will be less successful as chess players but that men *can* be just as successful as child-rearers, and that the feminists who insist that child-rearing is a learned rather than a biological role are providing an argument not for women's liberation, but for men's liberation.

According to Dr. Lee Salk, director of pediatric psychology at the New York Hospital-Cornell Medical Center, "Males clearly have the same instincts, the same protective feelings toward children as females have. . . . There is no scientific basis whatsoever to indicate that the female is superior in doing this (sc. caring for children)." According to Professor Eleanor Maccoby, chairman of Stanford's Psychology Department, there is little evidence that fathers are less responsive to infants. Fathers seem to show just as much nurturant behavior as mothers.[33]

Hear feminist therapist Elizabeth Friar Williams on the subject of motherhood:

Being a mother sounded like a great idea as she was growing up, but she was never told that the reality of motherhood for a particular woman might stink. . . . When I think of all the different personalities, talents, and yearnings that mothers may have and then think of all the different personalities that kids may develop, it seems totally absurd that we are taught from our own infancies that no matter who *we* are, no matter who *they* are, we're going to love our children and love caring for them!

Some women are able to say, "Okay, I don't like this scene or this kid, so I'm going to make the best of a bad thing by getting myself a good job that will take me out of the house during the day and a good housekeeper who does like taking care of children, and then nobody will suffer unduly. . . ." Well, these are not usually the mothers who come to psychotherapy.[34]

Men should be grateful for this agreement between feminists and psychologists that the system by which ex-wives use children as hostages to exploit ex-husbands is without biological or rational basis.

The untruthful assertion is commonly made by feminists that few fathers want custody of their children—commonly made, that is, by those who also commonly quote Engels to the effect that it was the yearning of men to perpetuate their patrimony through their offspring that led to the creation of the patriarchal family in the first place.[35]

The technique for hanging onto the meal ticket is well described by Metz:

This matter of leaving the home is a distinct liability in itself. Aside from the possible problem of the proper care of the children, your wife can and will at once call in her friends and relatives so that she can graphically show how truly she belongs in the home—her home, she says. She will also pointedly demonstrate how thoroughly capable she is of caring for the children—what a true little mother she is. In the home you made possible, she will also explain what a rotten person you are.

With a practiced tear in her eye and a trembling lip, she will be sure to mention how much she wanted the marriage to work. If she is the plaintiff, her witnesses will sop up this routine and swear undying allegiance. If she is the defendant, what better surroundings and background could she possibly get to secure assistance for her defense? Plaintiff or defendant, she only has to sit there, in the home, with the children, to illustrate how terrible it would be for anyone to try to take these things away from her. She may never have been worth a nickel as a wife or a mother, but she is sitting in the psychological driver's seat now. She will intend to stay there, too.

Particularly if you are suing for custody of the children, Mother will take every opportunity to explain to the kids that you left the home. She will also give them ample schooling on how much better and more normal ("usual" would be a better word in the light of most court decisions) it is that they be with her. And of course, she will suggest that we always want it this way, don't we, kiddies? (You're my meal ticket, you know—without you, no support payments. Maybe not even alimony.)[36]

The crucial consideration is this: giving custody to fathers provides no incentive to divorce; giving custody to mothers and subsidizing them with alimony and child-support payments gives wives powerful psychological gratifications and large fiscal rewards for divorce.

NOTES

1. 1835 edition, p. 66.
2. *Essays on Sex Equality,* ed. Rossi, p. 61. Rossi comments: "At the time he wrote women had no legal right to their own children." Mill, thou shouldst be living at this hour.

Mill, incidentally, hated his father with a deep intensity, a fact which must be considered in connection with everything this otherwise most rational of men wrote about the man-woman business.

3. Ruth Benedict, *The Chrysanthemum and the Sword*, p. 121.

4. 11b, *Parent and Child*, p. 638; quoted by R. F. Doyle, *The Rape of the Male*, p. 87.

5. Doyle, *loc. cit.*

6. Jeanne Cambrai, *Once Is Enough*. New York, Manor Books, 1974, pp. 8ff. According to Cambrai, there are two kinds of lawyers, *settlers* (for those husbands who are "generous and understanding,") and *fighters* who will go all out for you regardless of the cost (paid of course by the husband). "A lawyer like this can bring a woman out of a divorce with a terrific settlement but (translation: *and*) her husband may be left financially hog-tied. . . . If you really want blood and every penny that can be wrung out of the man, this is the lawyer for you."

7. This is called "standing on your own feet."

8. But which she consented to take.

9. Translation: Assert yourself, if you are female, as a deserving woman. Men should not assert themselves since they are not deserving.

10. Since you are entitled to the same benefits from the institution of divorce as from the institution of marriage. According to the Virginia Supreme Court (*Butler vs. Butler*, 9/2/76) "The rule applicable here requires a husband, within the limits of his financial ability, to maintain his former wife in a manner to which she was accustomed during the marriage." Nothing is said about her ability to earn or her ex-husband's right to offer his earnings to a possible second wife.

11. *Till Divorce Do You Part*, p. 37. "Independence" means, of course, "dependence without reciprocal responsibilities."

12. Cited in *The Liberator*, January, 1977.

13. Susan G. Ross, *The Rights of Women: The Basic ACLU Guide to Women's Rights*. New York, Avon Books, 1973, p. 217.

14. *Sexual Suicide*, p. 100.

15. *The Rape of the Male*, p. 92.

16. Ross, p. 221.

17. I am tempted to cite some of the horror stories given by R. F. Doyle in *The Rape of the Male,* pp. 93ff., but doing so might suggest that Ms. Ross was, relatively speaking, not so outrageous after all. My point is that any alimony and child-support payments are unjust as well as socially destructive. Doyle's point is that there is absolutely no limit to the anti-male discrimination of judges.

18. *Syracuse New Times,* 10 October 1976. This business about husbands being guilty of raping their wives can only be viewed by men's liberationists with amused satisfaction. Can you imagine courts, which are hardly ever able to convict strangers of rape, finding husbands guilty of it?

19. Neil Elliott, *Sensuality in Scandinavia.* New York, Weybright and Talley, 1970, pp. 91f. The Scandinavian women are almost as liberated as the women of our ghettos. The plight of the men is another matter. According to Elliott, boys are four times as likely as girls to come to the Association for Sex Information for psychiatric help. (p. 85)

Elliott's whole book should be read by anyone inclined to accept the feminist laudation of Scandinavian feminism.

20. *Ibid.,* p. 87.

21. *Subjugation of Women,* ed. Rossi, p. 217.

22. The phrases "*man is . . . an economic prey*" and "the masculine *idea of women as property*" occur within nine lines of each other. One who reads feminist literature gets used to this sort of thing.

23. *Masculine/Feminine,* p. 302.

24. Cox vs. Cox, Utah Supreme Court 3/6/75; cited by Doyle, p. 87.

25. *Beyond the Best Interests of the Child,* p. 40.

26. *Ibid.,* p. 42.

27. *Ibid.,* p. 35.

28. Metz, *Divorce and Custody for Men,* p. 41.

29. In Florence Howe, *Women and the Power to Change.* New York, McGraw-Hill Book Co., 1975, pp. 117f.

30. Cited in the *Newsletter of the Society of Single Fathers,* March 1977.

31. *Ibid.,* p. 31.

32. *Sexual Politics,* p. 225.

33. Cited by Doyle, p. 192.

34. Elizabeth Friar Williams, *Notes of a Feminist Therapist*. New York, Praeger Publishers, p. 77.

35. Engels is of course discredited. See, for example, Steven Goldberg, *The Inevitability of Patriarchy*, p. 52.

36. *Divorce and Custody for Men*, p. 48.

IV

The Fatherless Family

75% of delinquents and most adult criminals
are from broken homes. More than two-
thirds of criminal minors handled by the
Florida Division of Youth Services are from
broken homes. In Baltimore, Md., 60% of
juvenile criminals are from broken homes....
Statistics show that an overwhelming pre-
ponderance of these offenders are from
mother-only environments.... Drs. Sheldon
and Eleanor Glueck found the delinquency
ratio of children living with mother only,
compared with living with father only, to be
about three to one.
                                    —The Liberator

FEW READERS WILL have heard of Richard Lawrence, Charles
Guiteau, Leon Czolgosz, John Schrank, or Giuseppe Zangara.
These gentlemen were the assassins or attempted assas-
sins of Andrew Jackson, James Garfield, William McKinley,
Theodore Roosevelt, and Franklin Roosevelt, respectively.
Some may recall the name of Dean Corll, the Houston mass-
murderer, and everyone recalls that of John Wilkes Booth. Lee
Harvey Oswald, James Earl Ray, Sirhan K. Sirhan, Charles
Manson, Andreas Baader, and Lynette Fromme are house-
hold words.

These people share an interesting biographical oddity.
They all grew up with no fathers in their daily lives. Their
fathers were absent because of death, divorce, work sched-
ule, or a very poor personal relationship. Assassination (in
contrast to ordinary murder) appears to be a kind of killing of
the father-image.

The family backgrounds of these people and the activities
for which they are best remembered are worth considering
together in connection with such feminist pronouncements

as the following: "The destruction of the family will not mean the destruction of society. . . . In countries where the divorce rate is high, society is not falling apart. . . . 'Momism' [meaning evidently the institution of the fatherless family] in many cultures is not considered a negative factor. . . . An absence of a father does not necessarily cause problems."[1]

Not necessarily—just frequently; just from the viewpoint of the statistician, the actuary, the sociologist, the boys' vice principal, the crime reporter, and the police. From their vantage point the connection between delinquency and fatherless families is quite clear. Here is the sort of thing these people find:

> A survey conducted in Leningrad among 500 juvenile delinquents showed that 267 of them were from families with single mothers.[2]

> Broken homes do relate to the frequency of delinquency. Further, if a home is broken, a child living with the mother is more likely to be delinquent than one for whom other arrangements are made.[3]

> The great majority of unmarried mothers come from homes dominated by the mother.[4]

> Societies with relatively low father availability have a higher rate of crime than do societies in which the father is relatively available.[5]

> The bases for most of this unhappiness, as we have shown, are laid in the childhood home. The principal instrument of their creation are [sic] women.[6]

> Lower class boys who lack father or other strong male figures . . . have a problem of finding male models to imitate. Rejecting female dominance at home and at school and the morality which they associate with women may be the means such boys use to assert their masculinity, and such assertion must be performed with a strong antithesis of femininity, namely by being physically aggressive. Being a bad boy . . . can become a posi-

tive goal if goodness is too closely identified with femininity.[7]

A certain constellation of conditions is highly conducive to the development of homosexuality in men. Within this group of determining factors, a number of Momistic conditions stand out, such as a passive, disinterested father and an overbearing mother. It is hardly possible to produce a male homosexual if the father is affectionate to his wife and son and supportive of the son's masculinity.[8]

A close-binding mother-son relationship, in the context of paternal deprivation, is a frequent factor contributing to difficulties in heterosexual relationships and in the etiology of male homosexuality.[9]

The frequency of loss of father due to divorce or separation in childhood was much higher for individuals suffering from neurosis, psychosis, or personality disorders than for a number of different comparison groups.[10]

Henry M. Graham, executive director of the Family Service Association of Indianapolis . . . advised me that practically all of the girls in a study he made of unwed mothers had poor relationships with their fathers.[11]

Promiscuity is very clearly linked with poverty and squalor, low intelligence and the almost complete absence of any positive family life. Parents are divorced, in the hospital, in prison or dead. . . . There is rarely a breadwinning father in the family. . . . Three of the girls under consideration had been married and were divorced, and a fourth married the father of her third child. Another married a widower several years later. All the others remained single, as far as is known.[12]

According to the Welfare Department, "illegitimate" births triple every year, while the mothers are getting statistically younger. According to Robert A. Sack, associate professor of obstetrics and gynecology at USC School of Medicine, one out of five girls will conceive an illegitimate child between her 13th and 19th birthdays.[13]

Many studies have suggested that father-absent children often act very immature and frequently have a high rate of severe behavior problems associated with school adjustment.[14]

The researchers found that when the (Army) officers travelled, their sons became disorganized and impulsive. They misbehaved in school, vandalized their neighborhoods and picked fights with other children. And the longer the fathers stayed away, the more disturbed and delinquent the sons became. The researchers concluded that the men provided a stability and restraint which their sons deeply missed.[15]

(W. B.) Miller . . . argued that most lower-class boys suffer from paternal deprivation and that their antisocial behavior is often an attempt to prove that they are masculine. Bacon, Child and Barry . . . found that father availability was negatively related to the amount of theft and personal crime. . . . Societies with a predominantly monogamous nuclear family structure tended to be rated low in the amount of theft and personal crime, whereas societies with a polygamous mother-child family structure tended to be rated high in both theft and personal crime. Following Miller's hypothesis, Bacon, Child and Barry suggested that such antisocial behavior was a reaction against a female-based household and an attempted assertion of masculinity. A large number of psychiatric referrals with the complaint of aggressive acting-out are made by mothers of preadolescent and adolescent father-absent boys, and clinical data suggest that sex role conflicts are frequent in such boys.[16]

67

Paternal deprivation is negatively related to the strength of the child's conscience development. . . . The quality of the father-child relationship seems to have a particular influence on whether the child takes responsibility for his own actions or acts as if his behavior is controlled by external forces.[17]

A lack of accurate time perception, which is often associated with difficulties in self-control, is common among father-absent individuals.[18]

The road to the fatherless society is signposted by regressive anxieties.[19]

Women with tendencies toward abnormality as measured by the MMPI show a lack of identification with their fathers. . . . Masculine women identify with their fathers less than feminine women . . . and identification with the father is more important in producing normal adjustment than is identification with the mother.[20]

Over and over, psychiatrists told us in much the same words: "I never saw a homosexual who had a good relationship with his father. . . . High crime rates have been traced to fatherless or mother-dominated homes in city slums and in the Deep South. Three Yale University researchers, surveying 48 non-literate societies, found that sons had high crime records where mothers raised children by themselves; the scientists concluded that the crimes were part of a search for masculinity which the boys could not find at home. And Dr. Frank Pedersen, a child psychologist at the National Institute of Mental Health, studying disturbed children of Army officers who were overseas for long periods of time, found that the disturbances worsened the longer the fathers were away. He reported:

"Children with fathers absent become more impulsive and appear to lose the capacity to delay their reactions. While in the past the father was thought of mainly as a provider, it now looks like

[sic] he has a very important emotional effect on the child, probably a crucial one in the case of a boy."[21]

Kare Bødal found that among youthful delinquents (the subjects consisting of 100 reform school pupils) at least half had grown up without any permanent or stable contact with their fathers. Where the mother is rejected as an authority figure and the young boy has no opportunity to establish contact with a father or a permanent father-substitute, it is quite conceivable that the norms and ideals of the gang will be overwhelming in their influence. And of course in many cases the gang itself will consist largely of boys lacking the internal control mechanisms which can best be developed by harmonious, consistent contact with the father.[22]

According to Shervert Frazer, who studied convicted murderers in Texas prisons, "They are males with an absence of a father symbol."[23]

During World War II, the armed services found themselves rejecting so many draftees as to consider the psychological condition of the young American male a matter of national security. The consensus of opinion among psychiatrists was that much of what was wrong with these young men was attributable to mothers. Dr. Edward Strecker, psychiatric consultant to the Army and Navy, maintained that the problem was the mothers who had been the central characters in the lives of the rejected men and also in the lives of those who were accepted by the armed services and who broke down under slight combat stress. Dr. Strecker described these mothers as "Moms"—sweet, doting and self-sacrificing, or else as domineering and overprotective types.

Each one, he concluded after contact with many products of their handiwork, finds in her children "ego satisfaction for life's thwartings and frustrations, neither appreciating nor understanding the havoc they will leave in their wakes."[24]

Most glue sniffers and streakers come from broken homes headed by women.[25] Auto insurance companies, aware of the influence of fatherless homes, charge far higher premiums for boys living in them.[26] According to Martin Gold, Chinese, Japanese, and Jews have maintained low delinquency rates despite discrimination and past poverty in part thanks to their scholarly traditions and partly because of their traditions of the patriarchal family.[27]

The immaturity of fatherless children appears to be related to Mom's perpetuation of maternal functions that preserve a child's immaturity in order that the mother's role may remain central. On this matter Hans Sebald has much of value to say in his book *Momism: The Silent Disease of America.* Thus:

> Unlike the overprotective mother, who suppresses the ego development of the child, the overindulgent mother focuses on his id forces; but rather than suppress the id (the hedonistic and selfish demands of the child), she caters to it. In seeing to the gratification of his egotistic demands, she establishes the offspring's tenacious dependence on her rather indiscriminate nurturing. . . . One of the important underlying needs of the overindulgent mother is her craving for the child's love and loyalty. This craving is often symptomized in forms that overlap the martyr type, where the mother tries to impress the child with her altruism, or even suffering, for him.[28]

The overindulgent mother achieves much the same result as the overprotective mother—a lack of individuality in the son, who grows up with a catered-to and engorged id, unprepared for life, unable to give and take in mature relationships. The child becomes addicted to his mother, but his superego is undeveloped. Sebald cites a case:

> He learned that his demands and temper tantrums got him everything he wanted. Instead of disciplining him and applying aversive reinforcement, his mother rewarded his unreasonable and egocentric

fits by extending "love" and giving in to whatever he wanted.[29]

It is pitiable to see such a child attempting to negotiate the transition from adolescence to adulthood, guided only by a mother who may have understood her maternal functions well enough in the boy's early life, but who continues acting towards him as though those maternal functions were still as essential as they formerly were, inhibiting the growth of his self-reliance and self-respect, driving him to break out in rebellion in his search for his masculine identity. He turns to tantrums, rages, and violent demonstrations that the mother cannot control and which she, in effect, encourages with her unconditional mother love—once the precondition of his growth, now a stumbling block. "Her boy," says Philip Wylie in one of the most memorable passages of his celebrated *Generation of Vipers,*

having been "protected" by her love, and carefully, even shudderingly, shielded from his logical development through his barbaric period, or childhood (so that he has either to become a barbarian as a man or else to spend most of his energy denying the barbarism that howls in his brain—an autonomous remnant of the youth he was forbidden) is cushioned against any major step in his progress toward maturity. Mom steals from the generation of women behind her (which she has, as a still further defense, also sterilized of integrity and courage) that part of her boy's personality which should have become the love of a female contemporary. Mom transmutes it into sentimentality for herself . . . as invidious a spiritual parasitism as any in the book. With her captive son or sons in a state of automatic adoration of herself (and just enough dubiety of their wives to keep them limp or querulous at home) Mom has ushered in the new form of American marriage: eternal ricochet. The oppositeness of the sexes provides enough of that without Mom's doubling of the dose

71

and loading of the dice, but Mom does it—for Mom. Her policy of protection, from the beginning, was not love of her boy but of herself, and as she found returns coming in from the disoriented young boy in smiles, pats, presents, praise, kisses, and all manner of childish representations of the real business, she moved on to possession.

. . . .

Mom's boy will be allowed to have his psychological struggle with Dad: to reach the day when he stands emotionally, toe-to-toe with his father and wins the slugging-out. That contest is as unavoidable as the ripening of an apple. It may last only a second—in which a young man says, "I will" and an older man says, "You will not," and the younger man does. And it is a struggle no youth can engage in, but only a youth who has reached full manhood. But if it occurs prematurely, as under Mom's ruinous aegis it usually does, it leads to more serfdom for the boy. He is too young for independence.

Thus the sixteen-year-old who tells his indignant dad that he, not dad, is going to have the car that night and takes it—while Mom looks on, dewy-eyed and anxious—has sold his soul to Mom and made himself into a lifelong sucking egg. His father, already well up the creek, loses in this process the stick with which he had been trying to paddle. It is here that Mom has thrust her oar into the very guts of man—and while she has made him think she is operating a gondola through the tunnels of love, and even believes it herself, she is actually taking tickets for the one-way ferry ride across the Styx.[30]

The defense will be made that Momism is the response of women cabined, cribbed, and confined into too narrow a sphere by the oppression of the patriarchal family—the oppression that inhibits their full flowering as human beings. The answer is that they are at least equally confined—and far poorer economically—as heads of fatherless families, in which all the burdens and cares of parenthood fall on their shoulders, and that such fatherless families produce not just distresses, afflictions, and vexations of the spirit to themselves but also a very large proportion of the pathology of society. The solution, as has been indicated, is to liberate these women from *all* the responsibilities of parenthood in cases of divorce, and to place their children in the custody of their fathers.

Hear Kate Millett as she unwittingly testifies to the stabilizing influence of patriarchy:

> We are not accustomed to associate patriarchy with force. So perfect is its system of socialization, so complete the general assent to its values, so long and so universally has it prevailed in human society, that it scarcely seems to require violent implementation.[31]

That's right, Kate. Patriarchy maintains the law and order of the realm. The skyrocketing divorce rate of the last decade and a half, with its creation of millions of fatherless families, has been accompanied by a skyrocketing delinquency rate. Not to mention the accompanying rise of feminism, with its encouragement of divorce. There were twice as many fatherless families in 1976 as in 1971.[32] "Because evisceration of his authority has left the married father with very little control, and the divorced father with none," writes R. F. Doyle, "we are witnessing the advent of a chaotic reign of youth. We see it everywhere, from the 'children's rights' movement to the pushing, grabbing, sneering teenagers encountered in every city and town. . . ." "Modern attitudes," he continues,

> have contaminated even Chinese-American communities, traditional abodes of unquestioned parental respect, and one of the last vestiges of realistically-structured families. Consequently, these children also are joining the ranks of delinquents, a trend formerly unheard of in these, or any male-dominated communities.[33]

The Children's Rights movement of which Doyle speaks is worth a comment. These children, who express their obligations to the homosexual Mattachine Society, issue such publications as "The Schoolstopper's Textbook," "Eighty-Seven Ways to Send Your Principal to the Funny-Farm. Some of the most imaginative tactics ever discovered by day-dreaming students are collected in this volume. Hundreds of testimonials have been received from satisfied organizers." Another is "Youth Liberation: News, Politics and Survival Information—Some of the best articles from the early issues of *FPS* (F—— Public Schools) are collected in this book, which was published by Times Change Press in 1972. It also contains the original Youth Liberation platform and personal statements from young people about their discovery of ageism and the need to struggle for liberation." Another publication: *Growing Up Gay,* "A dozen articles by sensitive young men and women about the experience of being young and gay. Included are articles about accepting one's gayness, coming out, and talking with parents. There is an extensive list of resources." *Growing Up Gay* "is an eloquent account of the kind of pain and beauty that every young homosexual lives with from day to day." It has on its cover a crude drawing of youngsters cuddling together in bed. Other publications are "'Teaching and Rebellion," "How to Start a High School Underground Paper," and "Young People and the Law."

PHILADELPHIA STUDENTS
DEMONSTRATE FOR GAY RIGHTS

Mademoiselle Simone de Beauvoir, one of the most enlightened of the feminists, who gave up the possibility of marriage and maternity to live the life of a bluestocking, tells of a recurring and baffling nightmare that long plagued her, a nightmare in which she visualized eggs and darning needles, the sight of which filled her with a bewildering horror. This clever lady, with all her learning and slick intellectualism, was incapable of figuring out that eggs are incipient life and that darning needles are implements commonly employed by women to abort this incipient life in themselves. She was incapable of figuring this out, that is to say, while she was awake; but it was obvious to her when she closed her books, fell asleep, and came into communication with her own deeper, wiser self that the life-style which she had chosen—foregoing marriage and maternity for what she calls (in the jargon she picked up from Sartre) the life of a "truly free existent"—that such a life-style was indeed a nightmare.

The feminist attempts to downgrade marriage and childbearing and to persuade women that career elitism is more important than motherhood—these are by no means new. According to Lenin,

> In all civilized countries, even the most advanced, the position of women is such as justifies their being called domestic slaves. Not in a single capitalist country, not even in the freest republic, do women enjoy complete equality.
>
> The aim of the Soviet Republic is to abolish, in the first place, all restrictions of the rights of women. . . . Our new law wiped out, for the first time in history, all that made women inferior. . . .
>
> Up to the present the position of women has been such that it is called a position of slavery. Women are crushed by their domestic drudgery, and only socialism can relieve them from this drudgery, when we shall pass from small household economy to social economy and to social tilling of the soil.
>
> Only then will women be fully free and emancipated. It is a difficult task.
>
> It has been observed in the experience of all liberation movements that the success of a revolution depends on the extent to which women take part in it. The Soviet government will help them. Our cause is invincible.[34]

It is the boast of the present Soviet government that "among the greatest achievements of the socialist system is the resolved female question"[35]—so that there are now women stevedores, miners, stokers, steel smelters, stone masons, cement workers, plasterers, painters, carpenters, whalers, and diggers—and Soviet men complain, in the words of one of them, that "men are getting fed up with crude women who have the manners of cowboys. Their bossy shouts around the house, their shabby way of dressing and their swaggering way of drinking bottoms-up like a man turns the home into a crude barracks. . . . And their language—not just on construction sites but in offices— makes even strong men blush."[36]

Feminists who tell us that fifty-four percent of the "intellectual workers" of the USSR, including three-quarters of the doctors, are women, don't tell us that "intellectual workers" include salesman, barbers, and manicurists or that only five percent of the women of the USSR receive a higher education or that female doctors are paid less than skilled laborers.

Can you imagine delicate little Gloria Steinem hauling a hundred-pound sack of grain up a gangplank? This is not the kind of liberation and equality the feminist-elitist has in mind. If such were the lot of American women, as it is the lot of Soviet women, Ms. magazine would carry mottos proclaiming the sanctity of marriage and the home and would be filled with clamorous demands for protective legislation for women. Elegant patrician ladies like Ms. Steinem will leave the stevedoring, truck-driving, and street-sweeping to the likes of Sojourner Truth while they perform the equally necessary functions of holding down fifty-one senatorships, granting interviews, holding press conferences, and denouncing their oppression from behind microphones on lecture platforms. Some of them will assure us that arduous work is in any case superfluous:

> There is no human reason for . . . anyone to work.
> All non-creative jobs (practically all jobs now
> being done) could have been automated long ago,
> and in a moneyless society everyone can have as
> much of the best of everything as she wants.[37]

"As much of the best of everything as she wants"—such is liberation. It resembles a program of fleas to establish their independence of dogs, meaning they will do nothing in return for their room and board; they will refuse responsibility, they will repudiate the celebrated Legitimacy Principle enunciated by Bronislaw Malinowski:

> No child should be brought into the world without a man—and one man at that—assuming the role of sociological father. By this apparently consistent and universal prohibition (whose penalties vary by class and in accord with the expected operations of the double standard) patriarchy decrees that the status of the child and mother is primarily and ultimately dependent upon the male. And since it is not only his social status, but even his economic power upon which his dependents rely, the position of the masculine figure within the family—as without it—is materially, as well as ideologically, extremely strong.[38]

The system of welfare that has largely undermined the Legitimacy Principle in the inner cities and generated a ghetto illegitimacy rate in excess of fifty percent is now, in cooperation with feminism and the divorce courts, threatening to bring the same fate that subsidizes the destruction of the inner cities to the suburbs. It is time for society to stop wrecking itself by encouraging illegitimacy and divorce; to place illegitimate children up for adoption; to place children of divorce in the custody of their fathers. Families headed by fathers don't go on welfare; they pay their own way. The only people who would suffer from this arrangement would be the lawyers who pocket billions of dollars in fees by helping to wreck families.

NOTES

1. *CSULA University Times*, 10 November 1976.
2. Kurganoff, *Women in the USSR*, p. 148.
3. Starke Hathaway and Elio Monachesi, *Adolescent Personality and Behavior*. Minneapolis, University of Minnesota Press, 1963, p. 81.

4. Leontine Young, cited in Pochin, *Without a Wedding Ring*, p. 7.

5. H. Biller, *Father, Child and Sex Role*, p. 38.

6. Ferdinand Lundberg and Marynia Farnham, *Modern Woman: The Lost Sex*, p. 71.

7. Marvin Wolfgang, in Gazell, *Youth, Crime and Society*, p. 47.

8. Hans Sebald, *Momism: The Silent Disease of America.* Chicago, Nelson-Hall, c. 1976, p. 184.

9. Biller, *Paternal Deprivation*, p. 94.

10. *Ibid.*, p. 81.

11. *Ibid.*, p. 79.

12. J. Pochin, *Without a Wedding Ring*, p. 35.

13. R. F. Doyle, *The Rape of the Male*, p. 78.

14. Henry Biller, *Paternal Deprivation.* Lexington, Mass., Lexington Books, 1974, p. 80.

15. Stanley Yolles, *Parade*, 20 June 1965.

16. Biller, *Paternal Deprivation*, p. 68.

17. *Ibid.*, p. 66.

18. *Loc. cit.*

19. Alexander Mitscherlich, *Society without the Father.* New York, Harcourt Brace and World, 1969, p. 303.

20. Biller, *Paternal Deprivation,* p. 120.

21. P. and B. Wyden, *Growing Up Straight.* New York, Stein and Day, 1968, pp. 61f.

22. Oer Olav Tiller in Edmund Dahlstrom, *The Changing Roles of Men and Women.* Boston, Beacon Press, 1967, p. 98.

23. Cited by Doyle, *The Rape of the Male,* p. 146.

24. Cited in *The Liberator,* May 1976. Doyle, p. 243, cites Dr. Danilo Ponce's view that fathers should have custody of boys after age three and girls after age eleven.

Ponce's views were expressed before the publication of Goldstein, Freud and Solnit's major work *Beyond the Best Interests of the Child*—with its powerful evidence concerning the deleterious effects of breaking the continuity of relationships with a caring parent (not necessarily the biological "parent"). It would be interesting to know whether Ponce has changed his views in the light of this book. Children do not grow younger, and maternal custody for even young children will mean either that the continuity of relationships must be broken or that the child will end up in the custody of the (probably) less desirable parent.

25. Doyle, p. 145.

26. *Ibid.*, p. 146.

27. Martin Gold, *Status Forces in Delinquent Boys*, p. 186.

28. *Momism*, pp. 141f.

29. *Ibid.*, p. 143.

30. Quoted in Adams and Briscoe, *Up Against the Wall, Mother*, pp. 89f.

31. *Sexual Politics.* New York, Avon Books, 1969, p. 43.

32. *Los Angeles Times*, 14 April 1976.

33. Doyle, p. 142.

34. Lenin, "Women and Society," in *The Woman Question*, p. 42.

35. Kurganoff, *Women in the USSR*, p. 5.

36. *Los Angeles Times*, 27 November 1976.

37. Valarie Solanas, *The SCUM Manifesto*, p. 36. SCUM is an acronym for the *Society for Cutting Up Men.* Solanas is the woman who nearly killed Andy Warhol.

38. *Sex, Culture and Myth*, p. 63.

V

The Double Standard

For years, feminists have railed against the sexual freedom of men and the double standard in morals, but now that the sexual revolution is here, they don't like it. Robin Morgan, a founder of W.I.T.C.H., is only one of those who claim that the new sexual freedom "never helped us—just made us more available," and someone else has written, "Women have gone from private property to public property—[sic] fair game."
                              —Helen Lawrenson

THE DOUBLE STANDARD. The phrase is understood to refer to the moral superiority of the female and to point up the contrast between her foul-mouthed, brutal, unshaved and unwashed husband—playing shuffleboard and getting drunk at the local pub—and her own loyalty, her loving and caring and faithfulness, her long-suffering, her weary and anxious vigils over the little ones—loving, enduring, submitting, even as the Apostle Paul bade her love, endure, and submit (Ephesians 5:22).

"What a mother's care means to her children has been so much romanticized and poetized," we are informed by Judge Musmano of the Pennsylvania Supreme Court, "that its substance has sometimes been lost in the flowers of rhetoric, in the aureole of song, and in the vivid color and glistening marble of painting and sculpture." The good judge is not without a pretty garland of the flowers of rhetoric himself, as may be seen from what follows, in which he almost rises from speech into song:

A mother's care means instruction in religion and morals, it means the inculcation of patriotism and love of country, it means the maintenance of a clean heart, it means the imparting of lessons on duties in citizenship, courtesy and good will to one's fellow-man, it means the practical things of preparing healthful food and the mending and repair of clothing, it means ceaseless vigil and the balm of the healing hand when fever visits and the virus strikes—it means all these things and a million others, from all of which the child grows up resolved that he may never be unworthy of the lessons learned at the knee of his most loving companion, his best teacher, his most devoted defender, and his greatest inspiration for this and the life to come, his blessed mother.[1]

A pretty picture for Mother's Day. Let's examine it.

Reader, can you recall the last time you heard a hostile joke concerning fathers-in-law? Have you, in fact, ever heard one? One suspects not. There are familial relationships concerning which hostile jokes are composed, but they are not composed about fathers-in-law. Concerning the general antipathy towards mothers-in-law, we have been provided with the following explanation by Mlle. Simone de Beauvoir, the great sage of feminism:

A certain masked horror of maternity survives, however. It is of especial interest to note that since the Middle Ages a secondary myth has been in existence, permitting free expression of this repugnance: it is the myth of the Mother-in-Law. From fable to vaudeville, man flouts maternity in general through his wife's mother, whom no taboo protects. He loathes the thought that the woman he loves should have been engendered: his mother-in-law is the visible image of the decrepitude to which she has doomed her daughter in bringing her forth. Her fat and wrinkles coming to the young bride whose future is thus mournfully prefigured, at her mother's side she seems no longer like an individual, but like a phase of a species; she is no longer the wished-for prey, the cherished companion, because her individual and separate existence merges into universal life. Her individuality is derisively contested by generality, the autonomy of her spirit by her being rooted in the past and in the flesh: it is this derision to which man gives objective existence in a grotesque personage.[2]

It will be a sufficient refutation of Mlle. de Beauvoir to point out that her argument is based on the supposition that only maternal mothers-in-law are hated, whereas it is a matter of common observation that the hatred of wives towards their husbands' mothers is no less than the hatred of husbands towards their wives' mothers—a consideration that might have suggested itself to someone considerably less clever than Mlle. de Beauvoir if that person had been interested in the truth rather than in special pleading. In fact there is reason for supposing that the myth of the mother-in-law is no myth; and, since most women become mothers-in-law, the question deserves to be considered whether that which is nonmythical about mothers-in-law might not be nonmythical about women in general.

Double standard indeed. Which sex is less inclined to gossip and backbite? Is it more likely that a man or a woman will cut in front of you in a queue? Hear Philip Wylie:

Much of the psychological material which got me studying this matter of moms came into my possession as I watched the flowerhatted goddesses battle over fabric [in department store sales]. I have seen the rich and the poor, the well-dressed and the shabby, the educated and the unlettered, tear into the stacked remnants day after day, shoving and harassing, trampling each other's feet, knocking hats, coiffures and glasses awry, cackling, screaming, bellowing and giving the elbow, without any differential of behavior no matter how you sliced them. I have watched them deliberately drive quiet clerks out of their heads and their jobs and heard them whoop over the success of the stratagem. I have seen them cheat and steal and lie and rage and whip and harry and stampede—not just a few women but thousands and thousands and thousands, from everywhere. I know the magnitude of their rationalizing ability down to the last pale tint and I know the blackguard rapacity of them down to the last pennyworth.[3]

But to resume our comparisons. Who is more likely to return money to a clerk who has made an error? Which sex is more magnanimous? Which parent is more likely to instruct a child to lie about his age when buying a movie ticket? If your dog bites your neighbor's child, would you prefer to discuss the problem with the child's father or with his mother? If there is a prowler in the yard, who is expected to remove the boar-spear from the mantel and issue forth to confront him? If an employer requires a worker's presence in the middle of the night, would he be more likely to summon a male or a female employee? And if he called both, which one would be more likely to beg off on grounds of sickness or fatigue? When a couple buys a home or a car, which one is more concerned about the solidity of construction and the quality of its engineering and which is more concerned with flashy extras? Who is more likely to whiffle and fib? What would you think of a man who accepted alimony or child-support payments, or who invited his male friends to his home for a Tupperware party, an Avon cosmetics party, or a costume jewelry party, at which they were expected to make purchases so that their host could receive a trinket from the manufacturer? Is a husband or a wife more likely to steal towels, wash cloths, ashtrays, and Gideon Bibles from a hotel? Why is it notorious that, as Mlle. de Beauvoir says, "men and women alike hate to be under the orders of a woman; they always show more confidence in a man"?[4] Why is the term *prima donna* feminine even when it is used to refer to a male? Can it be said of women what Caroline Bird says of men: "Most men have been taught as boys that it is wrong to take advantage of a rival, particularly if the rival is a woman"?[5]

Ask a waitress whether men or women tip more generously. Ask a telephone operator or a clerk whether she is more frequently bullied and browbeaten by men or by women. Wife-beaters are husbands by definition, and since most husbands are stronger than most wives not too much is heard about husband-beating.[6] The contrast in the behavior of the two genders of spouses is one upon which feminists dwell lovingly and lingeringly. Child abuse is a subject upon which they dwell less lovingly and lingeringly, for most child-abusers—and the worst child-abusers—are mothers. (The next worst are the mothers' boyfriends.)

It is a commonplace among lawyers, themselves liars by profession, that when a woman is placed upon the witness stand she will lie without compunction. "For half so boldly kan there no man swere and lyen as a woman kan," says the Wife of Bath. "Deceit, weyping, spinning, God hath yive to women kyndely whil that they may lyve." "Honesty in women has not been considered important. . . . Truthfulness has not been considered important for women, as long as we have remained physically faithful to a man, or chaste," writes Adrienne Rich;[7] and it is this chastity that is referred to as a woman's *virtue,* from *vir,* meaning "man." "It is indeed," says H. L. Mencken, "an axiom of the bar that women invariably lie upon the stand, and the whole effort of a barrister who has one for a client is devoted to keeping her within bounds, that the obtuse suspicions of the male jury may not be unduly aroused." Schopenhauer even questioned whether women should be sworn as witnesses at all. The Laws of Manu prohibited women from giving testimony and the ancient Hebrews required that a woman's oath should be corroborated by her husband or her father (Numbers 30:4). "Women prisoners," writes Arno Karlen, "tend to see each other according to society's usual feminine stereotypes— untrustworthy, devious, less reliable than men."[8]

Hear an anonymous woman quoted by the house-male Michael Korda in his book *Male Chauvinism:*

> Why does having children, wearing a skirt, disqualify you from being a hundred percent real person? Men can say of each other, "His word's as

good as his bond," but has anybody ever said "*Her* word's as good as her bond"? An honest *man* is a guy who won't cheat you, who's on your side. An honest *woman* still means a girl who isn't a prostitute, or a prostitute who delivers value for money. "He took it like a man," well we know that means a guy with guts; "taking it like a woman" means having hysterics, acting up. "A man's man" is Clark Gable or Paul Newman, that kind of image; a "man's woman" is just a woman who keeps her mouth shut, and pours out admiration and affection without asking too much in return. As an advertising person, I can tell you that our *image* as women is so lousy that it doesn't matter how successful you become in business, you're still stuck with a set of attitudes that are like a brick wall, and that allow men to interfere in what you're doing and control your work and even get the credit for it, while still feeling that they're *protecting* you. The trouble with male chauvinists is that they don't even think they're our enemies. Deep down where it counts, they still think in terms of "helping the little woman," and if you act like a battle-ax or a buzz-saw, that just makes them feel more generous and "understanding."[9]

She supposes the problem to be one of image-*creating*, but the image she complains of is an earned one. What would you think of male writers who produced such books as feminist writers produce—with their leasings and prevarications, their irresponsible "research," their fudgings and whifflings? Can you imagine a serious book on Shakespeare by Germaine Greer, a serious work on anthropology by Evelyn Reed, a serious work of literary criticism by Kate Millett? These women would be entirely unknown if they wrote about anything other than sex.

Why do credit companies and banks prefer male customers? Why does the New Japan Securities Company refuse to conduct margin trading in behalf of women customers?[10]

"Any man who is so unfortunate as to have a serious controversy with a woman, say in the departments of finance, theology or amour," writes H. L. Mencken,

> must inevitably carry away from it a sense of having passed through a dangerous and almost gruesome experience. Women not only bite in the clinches; they bite even in open fighting; they have a dental reach, so to speak, of amazing length. No attack is so desperate that they will not undertake it, once they are aroused; no device is so unfair and horrifying that it stays them. In my early days, desiring to improve my prose, I served for a year or so as reporter for a newspaper in a police court, and during that time I heard perhaps four hundred cases of so-called wife-beating. The husbands, in their defense, almost invariably pleaded justification, and some of them told such tales of studied atrocity at the domestic hearth, both psychic and physical, that the learned magistrate discharged them with tears in his eyes and the very catchpolls in the courtroom had to blow their noses. . . . The fact puzzles no one who has had the same opportunity that I had to find out what goes on, year in and year out, behind the doors of apparently happy homes. A woman, if she hates her husband (and many of them do), can make life so sour and obnoxious to him that even death upon the gallows seems sweet by comparison.[11]

Mencken's remarks suggest a thought that deserves further consideration: Is not *machismo*, the childish swaggering of males, the invention of females, designed to cast themselves into the complementary *marianismo*-role of long-suffering and morally superior madonnas? Didn't the wives described by Mencken really wish to be beaten? He speaks of the "delight in martyrdom that one so often finds in women."

> They take a heavy, unhealthy pleasure in suffering; it subtly pleases them to be hard put upon; they like to picture themselves as slaughtered

saints. Thus they always find something to complain of. . . . This fact probably explains many mysterious divorces: the husband was not too bad, but too good. For public opinion among women, remember, does not favour the woman who is full of a placid contentment and has no masculine torts to report. . . . (W)hen two women talk of their husbands it is mainly atrocities that they describe.[12]

And then there is the colored photograph of the contusions, which can be treasured—and perhaps brought into court—as proof of her martyrdom.

Hear Angela Sergio, reviewing a book about three Portuguese feminists, *The Three Marias*:

These courageous authors dared expose the soft underbelly of macho arrogance with its weakness and ugliness, and they dared to explore the full body of female compassion, love and understanding with its tenderness and beauty.[13]

Concerning the tendency of women to assume "the role of victim," Simone de Beauvoir says: "This renunciation on the mother's part is easily reconciled with a tyrannical will to domination; the *mater dolorosa* forges from her sufferings a weapon that she uses sadistically."[14] Sociologists inform us that marriages between alcoholic husbands and long-suffering wives frequently break up if the husband gives up booze and thus prevents the wife from being a long-suffering martyr any more—prevents her friends and relatives from marveling at her sanctity and Griseldic patience, and from declaring "She's too good for him—I suppose she puts up with him for the children's sake." It's called role disturbance.

What a trip. "I became aware that Latin American women were more comfortable in their roles than their Anglo-American counterparts," writes Evelyn P. Stevens:

Latin American mestizo cultures—from the Rio Grande to the Tierra del Fuego—exhibit a well-defined pattern of beliefs and behavior centered on popular acceptance of a stereotype of the ideal woman. . . . Among the characteristics of this ideal are semidivinity, moral superiority, and spiritual strength. This spiritual strength engenders abnegation, that is, an infinite capacity for humility and sacrifice. No self-denial is too great for the Latin American woman, no limit can be divined to her vast store of patience with the men of her world. . . .

Beneath the submissiveness, however, lies the strength of her conviction—shared by the entire society—that men must be humored, for, after all, everyone knows that they are *como niños* (like little boys) whose intemperance, foolishness, and obstinacy must be forgiven because "they can't help the way they are."

. . . .

But to the unalterable imperfection of men is attributable another characteristic of Latin American women: their sadness. They know that male sinfulness dooms the entire sex to a prolonged stay in purgatory after death, and even the most diligent prayerfulness of loving female relatives can succeed in sparing them only a few millennia of torture.

. . . .

(T)he image of the black-clad mantilla-draped figure, kneeling before the altar, rosary in hand, praying for the souls of her sinful menfolk, dominates the television and cinema screens, the radio programs, and the popular literature, as well as the oral tradition of the whole culture area. This is Latin America's chief export product, according to one native wit.[15]

Corny—but it makes women feel appreciated and keeps men childlike.

In the context of this discussion of the female long-suffering act, a word should be said concerning the Equal

Rights Amendment. The ERA is superfluous: everything it stipulates is already provided by the Fourteenth Amendment; and the claim of the feminists and their house-males like Ashley Montagu that the Constitution says nothing specifically about the rights of females is comparable to a like complaint by redheads and left-handed folk concerning the Constitution's silence about their rights, and about the afflictions they suffer at the hands of brunette-chauvinists and dextral-chauvinists. But the main point to be made in the present connection is this: Just as battered wives generally provoke the attacks made upon themselves, so the feminists *want* the ERA to be rejected in order that they may point to such rejection as proof of their distress and of the injustice of society.

Enough. The fact is that in every area of behavior, with but a single exception, society expects and gets more responsible behavior from men than from women.[16] The exception exists for the obvious reason that a woman who is sexually promiscuous is undermining her own family, whereas a man who is sexually promiscuous is not. And because of this single exception we are subjected to anguished complaints about the injustice of the double standard which does not permit our wives to introduce confusion of progeny into our households. What gall. What procacity. *Mort du Vinaigre!* It out-chutzpahs chutzpah.

NOTES

1. *Commonwealth ex rel. Edinger v. Edinger* 6/26/53; quoted by Doyle, *The Rape of the Male,* p. 100.

2. Simone de Beauvoir, *The Second Sex.* New York, Alfred A. Knopf, 1953, p. 174.

3. Quoted in *Up Against the Wall, Mother,* p. 91.

4. *The Second Sex,* p. 135.

5. In *Up Against the Wall, Mother,* p. 297.

6. Perhaps more needs to be said about husband-beating. One hears that it is the most underreported crime in America, husbands being understandably reluctant to tell a smirking

police desk-sergeant that they cannot maintain order in their own homes. I have heard that 20% of husbands have been beaten by their wives. One would not have supposed that there were that many wives physically capable of it.

7. Adrienne Rich, *Women and Honor* (unpaginated).

8. *Sexuality and Homosexuality.* New York, W. W. Norton, 1971, p. 555.

9. Korda, *Male Chauvinism*, p. 128.

10. The New Japan Securities Co. says it will no longer carry on margin trading in behalf of women customers because they are a nuisance.

"We have had many problems," a spokesman for the firm said.

He said women customers:

—Refused to accept responsibility for transactions that turned out badly.

—Often accused the company of making purchases and sales without authorization.

—Played the market on the margin without knowledge of their husbands, and left strict orders that reports of their transactions never were to be mailed to their homes.

The firm said it was not against women's liberation and that exceptions would be made on a case-by-case basis for women doctors and attorneys and for women who ran businesses.

—*Los Angeles Times,* 29 October 1975.

11. *In Defense of Women*, p. 174.

12. *Ibid.,* p. 155.

13. Supplement to *The Other Woman*, 8 March 1977.

14. *The Second Sex*, p. 514.

15. Evelyn P. Stevens, "Marianismo: The Other Face of Machismo in Latin America." In *Female and Male in Latin America*, ed. Ann Pescatello.

16. We are informed by Betty Friedan that 40% of American wives are now practicing adultery. If this appalling figure is true (and it must be true if Betty Friedan says so), it is doubtful whether women behave more responsibly in any area whatever—though, be sure, much male chastity must be ascribed to the epidemic of sexual impotence that has taken place since the rise of feminism.

VI

The Oppression of Women

*We know that men stand a 500 percent
greater risk of a coronary than women, and,
in the past two decades, deaths from heart
attacks have jumped 14 percent among men
aged 25-44, while declining some 8 percent
among women in the same age group.*
—Harvey Kaye

DR. ALICE ROSSI, feminist and Professor of Sociology at
Goucher College, published an essay in 1969 in which she
discussed, among other things, why women do not form a
united front against men for the purpose of fighting male
oppression. She says:

> For a married woman to affiliate with an activist
> women's rights group might very well trigger ten-
> sion in her marriage. . . . A large proportion of mar-
> ried women [who] have not combated sex discrimi-
> nation . . . fear conflict with men, or [they] benefit in
> terms of a comfortable high status in exchange for
> economic dependence upon their husbands.[1]

Dig, if you will, the words "in exchange for." On the one
hand, the husband provides the wife with status by placing
her under coverture in the honorable estate of matrimony, by
permitting her to share in the dignity of his titles and honors.
And "in exchange" what does the wife do for the husband?

She assumes economic dependence upon him—permits *him* to pay *her* bills. This, in feminese, is an "exchange." And this, in feminese, is oppression.

What endless finger-wringings, grumblings, and repinings we find in feminist literature on the subject of the oppression of women. The *Redstocking Manifesto* describes women as an oppressed class—totally oppressed with an oppression affecting every aspect of their lives—oppressed and exploited as sex objects, breeders, servants, whose only purpose is to enhance men's lives. So oppressed that they do not even see their oppression and fail to comprehend its political nature—a view partly shared by Eleanor Holmes Norton and Linda Jenness. Caroline Lund thinks the oppression of the family grinds women down psychologically and gives them the mentality of slaves, makes them drudges and dependents; and she believes that women must demand that society shall provide them with the facilities to fulfill all their capacities and talents so that they may become complete human beings. Robin Morgan thinks that the primary oppression is that of being female in a patriarchal world, and she laments that even the sisters in the Gay Liberation Front are oppressed by, of all people, male homosexuals.

Barbara Burris is dismayed that there is no "analysis" of the imperialism and colonialism by which men exploit women, a situation especially acute since women have no ghetto into which they can flee. Sheila Cronan sneers that marriage "protects" women the way slave-owners "protected" blacks, a sentiment seconded by Ti-Grace Atkinson. Germaine Greer believes women are the most oppressed of all "classes" and that it is not too melodramatic to call them slaves. Joreen in the *Bitch Manifesto* declares that women are slaves and denounces society for condemning their slave-like behavior. Simone de Beauvoir considers the lot of wives so pitiable that marriage, like private property, should simply be prohibited.

Such is the complaint of the feminist—or such it is when she sits at her typewriter or stands behind a microphone on a lecture platform. A different complaint is heard, however, when she closes the soundproof door of her psychiatrist's office and unburdens herself to him. According to Dr. Karl Menninger, for every woman a psychiatrist hears complain about oppression by men, there are a dozen who complain about the dependency, passivity, and impotence of men.[2] According to Lawrence Fuchs, visitors to America from Asia, Europe, Africa, and South America, from the 18th century to the present, have regarded America as a woman's paradise and regarded American women as pampered, spoiled, assertive, powerful, and remarkably independent.[3]

The ancestresses of the feminists who are harrying us might have felt they had much to be liberated from. Apart from giving birth to, tending, and burying their children, their days were occupied in washing and wringing; harvesting the glebe; tending the pigpen, the chicken coop, the sheepfold and the stable; fetching wood; spading; picking fruit; preserving; pickling; cooking; sweeping the house with a broom made of twigs; mending clothes; and a thousand other labors. Men now in the prime of life can remember their mothers doing the family laundry on a washboard, sweeping the home with a broom, washing dishes with hot water from a kettle heated over a wood stove, storing food in a cooler, and listening to a crystal set radio. When their fathers were able to buy their mothers washing machines, for example, a heavy load was lifted from them—but they became somewhat less important, less indispensable persons. And it was the same with the other appliances and conveniences their fathers bought their mothers—all invented, engineered, manufactured, and purchased by men for the benefit of women.

Thanks to the labor of American men, the suburban American housewife today lives in a home for which the Queen of Sheba and Eleanor of Aquitaine would gladly have exchanged their palaces and their servants. Dr. William Stephens has truly said that our society treats its wives most generously. As Robert Ardrey observes, women today live in a feminine utopia. They control four-fifths of the buying power of the country and most advertisers court them over men. It has been estimated (by Beverly Jones) that American women spend one-twelfth of their lives—one-eighth of their waking lives—in grooming themselves. Their pampering by their husbands is a subject of merriment to the entire world, and it is acknowledged even by foreign feminists like Simone de Beauvoir.

It is not in the least paradoxical that these pampered

93

creatures should complain so much about their oppression. The spoiled child gets its way by pouting and throwing tantrums—and every feminist is, if not precisely a spoiled child, at least an elitist. Elizabeth Cady Stanton, the Betty Friedan of the 19th century, was resentful that women were forced to spend so much of their time conversing with children *and* servants. J. S. Mill wrote in his early *Essay on Marriage and Divorce,*

> We have all heard the vulgar talk that the proper employment of a wife are [sic] household superintendence and the education of her children. As for the household superintendence, if nothing be meant but merely seeing that servants do their duty, that is not an occupation; every women [sic] that is capable of doing it at all can do it without devoting anything like half an hour every day to that purpose. . . . [4]

Mill was too sensible to believe that all women had servants, but evidently he felt that having them was the natural condition of womankind, for he went on to speak of women without servants as doing "the work of servants."

In Rome a few years ago, there was a radio panel which included one feminist from Sweden and four from southern Europe. The Swede spoke first and denounced the oppression of women and the discrimination against them in her country. The other four all chanted the praises of their own societies and spoke of the wonderful way they treated women. The moderator who summarized the discussion expressed her astonishment that Swedish women, more pampered even (if such a thing is possible) than their American sisters, should be so bitter about the utopia of Ultima Thule, while the mamas from the patriarchal south were so happy. The explanation wrung from the Swedish feminist was that it was *because* Swedish women had advanced so far that they wanted to advance still farther.[5]

Lesbian-feminist-therapist Elizabeth Friar Williams believes that a woman isn't healthy unless she can support herself by work that is fun and that makes her feel competent. Failing this, she needs therapy.[6]

By such a definition most women, happy housewives included, are unhealthy—something that, if believed, might generate a lot of therapist fees but that will eliminate little frustration from the women who are convinced they need the therapy.

Lesbian-feminist Sharon Deevey had once been married to a husband who paid her bills, helped her with the dishes, and encouraged her interest in feminism. Thanks to the feminist meetings she attended, she came to a realization of how oppressed she was, that what she had supposed was "natural" was a damned lie, and that she could do something about it. She now understood that male supremacy was the source of all oppression and that a part of this oppression was the introjection of guilt feelings into her soul. She was going to put an end to all this oppression by taking up shoplifting in preparation for the women's revolution that would soon change the world, and by kicking her husband out of the house, which she did. Thereupon she cut her hair short, became a man-hating dyke and went to work for the revolution.[7]

So it goes with these distressed creatures. The consideration suggests itself that, while for polemical and panhandling purposes they lace their literature with talk about oppression, their real problem is what the she-Solomon Betty Friedan calls the problem that has no name.

There is, however, a name for the problem that has no name. It is "acedia"—the *tedium vitae* of idle ladies who spend most of their day holding coffee klatches, working crossword puzzles, reading magazines, meditating divorce, playing bridge, itinerating the department stores, and spending their husbands' paychecks. (In feminist agitprop this last is represented as exploitation by merchants and manufacturers, who villainously direct three-quarters of their advertising towards women. Isn't that precious?)

Acedia has nothing to do, as Ms. Friedan would have us believe, with the feminine mystique. It is a problem shared by many men and it is traditionally the affliction of monks in monasteries. It has been around a long time and is one of the seven deadly sins. You can read all about it in Burton's *Anatomy of Melancholy*.

Feminists have sought relief from their acedia, sought a sense of purpose in their lives, by undertaking programs to accomplish such goals as the destruction of the family. The words of Ms. Friedan cited at the beginning of the book merit repetition:

> The changes necessary to bring about equality were, and still are, very revolutionary indeed. They involve a sex-role revolution for men and women which will restructure all our institutions: child rearing, education, marriage, the family, medicine, work, politics, the economy, religion, psychological theory, human sexuality, morality, and the very evolution of the race.[8]

Such a program should relieve boredom for a while and elevate feminists to a level of importance above that provided by their merely reproductive functions. Simone de Beauvoir believes that conserving and continuing the world as it is seems undesirable. The male acts, fights, creates, progresses, and transcends himself towards the totality of the universe and the future. The female can't do this because she is held down by her reproductive functions and by the confounded institution of marriage. Marriage, therefore, must go. The downgrading of marriage and maternity is the endlessly repeated theme of such books as the O'Neills' oafish and lubberly *Open Marriage* and of a hundred other confused feminist tracts.

Can marriage and the family be abolished without destroying society? One recalls Bronislaw Malinowski's view that if this ever happened we would be faced with a social catastrophe that would make such things as the French Revolution and the rise of communism appear insignificant.

In any case, the feminists' grasping after what they deem male perks is motivated by a mistake: they have confused *rights* with *status*, and focused all their attention and energies on the former, which they hope to acquire by pressuring politicians and bureaucrats, and by assaulting the public with clamors and tumults. Yet males continue to hold as many high-status positions as ever; and a principal result of the feminist downgrading of the maternal functions which only a woman can perform and which are the principal source of female status has been to lessen the status of the great majority of women, who are housewives and mothers. The real liberation of women is to be achieved by acknowledging the importance of maternal functions.

Another principal source of female status is provided by husbands. If society could decree that status could not be conferred upon women by marriage and by the achievements of husbands, then both the status of women and the motivation of men would be lowered further. To put it differently, high status for women requires the patriarchal family.[9]

NOTES

1. In Roszak, *Masculine/Feminine*, pp. 178f. Originally published as "Sex Equality: The Beginning of Ideology," *The Humanist*, Sept./Oct., 1969.

2. *Saturday Review of Literature*, April 1953.

3. *Family Matters*, p. 90.

4. Edited by F. A. Hayek in *John Stuart Mill and Harriet Taylor*, p. 66.

5. Anna-Greta Leijon, *Swedish Women—Swedish Men*, p. 30.

6. *Notes of a Feminist Therapist*, p. 9.

7. *Lesbianism and the Women's Movement*, pp. 21ff.

8. *New York Times Magazine*, 4 March 1973.

9. The subject of status is well treated by Steven Goldberg in *The Inevitability of Patriarchy*. Feminists could save themselves much anguish by studying this book.

VII

Affirmative Action

Of these chairmen . . . thirty-two percent reported they had felt coerced to hire a woman or a minority member regardless of whether or not he or she was the best candidate for the job.

—Nathan Glazer

On these economic questions the feminists are right in virtually every superficial way. Married men, at least, do earn more than women; women are discouraged from competing with men; when sufficiently motivated, women individually can perform almost every important job in the society as well as men; job assignments by sex are arbitrary and illogical; most women do work because they have to; the lack of public child-care facilities does prevent women from achieving real financial equality of opportunity.

But at a profounder level the women are tragically wrong. For they fail to understand their own sexual power; and they fail to perceive the sexual constitution of our society, or if they see it, they underestimate its importance to our civilization and to their own interest in order and stability.

—George Gilder

ONE WONDERS HOW many people who profess sympathy with feminism have read such books as George Gilder's *Sexual Suicide*, George Roche's *The Balancing Act*, Nathan Glazer's *Affirmative Discrimination*, or R. F. Doyle's *The Rape of the Male*, books that explain how the feminist program—

affirmative action, free day-care centers, E.R.A., divorce subsidized by husbands, the abandoning of the rational socialization of children, and so forth—works to undermine the family and civilized society.

The present chapter is concerned with the first of these, affirmative action.

The university where I teach recently joined the hue and cry for what is designated by the Orwellian expression "Equal Opportunity/Affirmative Action." The solidus between the two halves of the expression is intended to mean that my university believes in both of the stated principles: Equal Opportunity and Affirmative Action. If, however, one translates the name of this program out of Orwellese into plain English one finds that the translation of "Equal Opportunity" is "You will be employed, paid, and promoted on the basis of merit, motivation, and achievement," and the translation of "Affirmative Action" is "If you are a member of an unsuccessful group, a government bureaucracy will reward you for your membership in that unsuccessful group and will finance your reward by discrimination against Caucasian males." No person of integrity should affect to believe that these two contradictory policies are capable of being reconciled and combined into one.

It is perhaps to the credit of feminists, in one sense, that they do not even profess to demand Equal Opportunity. Here is Linda Jenness, the Socialist Workers' Party candidate for President in 1972. Writing of "women and Blacks and other oppressed nationalities [sic]" and asserting that the plight of blacks is "just as dismal" as that of women, she says:

> One proposal is that recently hired women and Blacks be given preferential seniority. That is, although only recently hired, they would automatically be given a higher seniority rating as partial compensation for past discrimination and as partial protection against layoffs.
>
> This is only fair. It is hardly the fault of Blacks and women that they are the last hired, so they should not be forced to suffer under the "last hired, first fired" rule.

And then this:

> Special seniority provisions are not new to the union movement. Ever since World War II, for example, some unions have guaranteed men drafted into war their jobs upon return. In addition to their jobs, they were given the seniority they would have earned had they not been drafted.
> Another proposal is to insist that layoffs cannot be used to reduce the percentage of women or Blacks in a particular workplace. In other words, this means preserving a minimum quota of jobs for Blacks and women.[1]

As though a woman, by virtue of her nonsuccess on the job market, were entitled to the same gratitude from society as a soldier who had given years of his life for the benefit of his country while others remained at home safely earning fat paychecks.

According to a feminist publication called *Spinning Off,*

> WOMEN-OWNED BUSINESSES are being sought for contracting by the LOS ANGELES UNIFIED SCHOOL DISTRICT. The District buys everything from data processing equipment, paint and maintenance supplies to vehicles, dry goods and printing materials. For information call Betty Miller 625-5115 or Daryl Freeman, 625-5256.

Women-owned businesses, that is to say, are being sought by feminists and house-males who have crept, climbed, and intruded themselves into the fold of the Los Angeles School District and who feel themselves entitled to break the law by using the taxpayers' money to discriminate on the basis of sex. To borrow the words of Linda Jenness, this is only fair.

According to Professor Thomas Sowell of UCLA, himself a black, "If the 'affirmative action' program were merely inane, futile, and costly, it might deserve no more attention than other government programs of the same description. But it has side effects which are negative in the short run and perhaps poisonous in the long run." He goes on:

100

While doing little or nothing to advance the position of minorities and females, it creates the impression that the hard-won *achievements* of these groups are conferred benefits. Especially in the case of Blacks, this means *perpetuating* racism instead of allowing it to die a natural death or to fall before the march of millions of people advancing on all economic fronts in the wake of "equal opportunity" laws and changing public opinion.[2]

According to the same publication, The Public Interest, Winter 1976, single men professors earn less than single women professors, and black professors have higher incomes than similarly qualified whites.

The fact is that discrimination does not exist on college campuses—or did not until the introduction of affirmative action programs whose beneficiaries are underqualified people and the parasitic bureaucrats who run these programs: people like J. Stanley Pottinger and his pestilential hustlers and carpetbaggers in HEW and other federal agencies.[3] According to one of these hustlers, a Labor Department lawyer named David P. Callett,

> Federal guidelines for affirmative action programs
> . . . require . . . that employers use special standards when considering women and minority group members, and, if necessary, educate and train them so that they will be able to compete effectively for jobs. . . .
> It is when employers design their programs as a matter of expediency, rather than *spend the extra time and money to seek out* qualified women and minority group applicants, that court challenges arise.[4]

In other words, men, most of them breadwinners for families, are to lose out on jobs to women so unmotivated that they haven't even bothered to apply for them. We need affirmative action the way we need green golf balls.

101

According to an article in the *Los Angeles Times* of 17 May 1978, the carpetbagging Equal Employment Opportunity Commission, "long viewed as one of the most dismal failures in the entire federal bureaucracy," has recently "received another critical vote of confidence when President Carter chose the commission to become the centerpiece of the government's newly streamlined fair employment system, giving the agency greater clout and additional enforcement responsibilities," which permit it to take over affirmative programs from the Labor Department and the Civil Service, the principal government branches still fighting to maintain a meritocracy. This is now enabling EEOC, under its new director Eleanor Holmes Norton, to disregard much of its 130,000 backlog of complaint cases, which the Commission was created to decide on the basis of their merits, and to expand "individual complaints into broader class-action court suits." Instead of tediously and judiciously ascertaining whether a complaint has merit, Mrs. Norton, who complains that "the business community—those companies that illegally discriminate—has never had to take this commission seriously," can now sweep aside individual complaints (in which employers were presumed to have a right to a hearing) by largely relying on expanding individual complaints into broader class-action court suits—and "challenging employment trends for entire industries rather than focusing on individual firms." "I think businessmen who see such a serious, relentless litigation program under way will soon get the message that we mean business, and they had better start changing some things," says Mrs. Norton. The business community has evidently gotten the message, bitten the bullet, and decided that their claims to equity are not going to be considered by the carpetbaggers at EEOC, and that they had better pay the blackmail and protection money.

Another similar agency is the Office of Federal Contract Compliance Programs (OFCCP), which specializes in "taking contracts away from companies that refuse to comply with federal discrimination laws." In the first few months after OFCCP was taken over by its new head, Weldon Rougeau, contracts totaling $150 million were canceled. Previously, according to Rougeau, the bureau was "something of a joke. It was not respected. That cannot and will not continue."

Rougeau, a black, boasts that he has vast powers and means to use them. "We'll have about 20 or more cases within another year, with contracts that could cost the companies hundreds of millions of dollars."[5]

Faced with such pressures, most employers, even corporate giants, are simply paying the money, often without admitting guilt, and instituting quotas.

According to the feminist house-male Frank Askin, "There is nothing in law, logic, or morality which requires, as a neutral principle, equivalent treatment of oppressor and oppressed.[6] And from this premise a feminist named Wallach reasons as follows:

> If Askin's criterion is applied to the case of compensatory treatment of women, the proper test for such benign sex classification is not the emergent test of presumptive invalidity, but rather the traditional equal protection test of reasonableness of the classification, under which *preferential treatment of women would be permissible even though discrimination against women would still be presumptively invalid.*[7]

Here is the way this nondiscrimination works out:

> Any adequate concept of equality, as applied to the need for all-women law firms must include the right of all-women law firms to refuse to hire qualified male attorneys, because the liberation of women requires it. At the same time it must forbid all-men law firms to refuse to hire qualified female attorneys. Both of these positions are justifiable as necessary to the eventual attainment of equality by an oppressed and colonialized class—women— and until such time as women will have achieved the condition of *real* parity with all men. In the meantime, parity between the sexes is insufficient because it cannot yield equality.[8]

It is best not to reply to such an argument. The purpose of argumentation is to make something clearer than it was previously, and nothing can be clearer than the fact that this impudence is the very opposite of a plea for equal opportunity.

Discrimination against women is a myth. If one asks for evidence of it he will be given the familiar assertions that women earn little more than half of what men earn; that there are no women senators or Supreme Court justices; and that the higher paying positions in all professions are mostly held by men.

It is intelligible that women would like more money and that, like other relatively less successful elements of the population, they should turn to government bureaucracies in an attempt to get it. But there is one thing in their argument that remains unintelligible: How is their conclusion that women are discriminated against presumed to be derived from their premise that women are less successful than men? If there is a race between two runners and one runner comes to the finish line far ahead of the other, why may not the inference be made that the winner is the swifter runner? Why should it be supposed that the loser has lost because of unfair discrimination, and that the winner ought therefore to carry a handicap so that both runners will in future reach the finish line simultaneously?

Of course most men make more money than most women. How could it be otherwise? Most men have wives, who perform innumerable services for them. An employer who hires a married man is engaging the services of two people. Most married men have children for whom they wish, and by whom they are expected, to provide the good things of life. Men with such advantages and such motivation are most certainly going to earn more than those—women and single men—who lack them. It is well for society that they should—and that they should teach their sons to expect to do the same when they becomes husbands and fathers. Women, in fact, do not earn a mere 60 percent of what men earn, as the feminists allege. They earn 60 percent of what *married* men earn—and almost exactly the same as what single men earn. Actually slightly more.[9]

Put it this way: it is well that male aggression should be employed for useful purposes. It is the squandered aggression of single males, improperly socialized by the civilizing

104

influence of the patriarchal family, that produces most crime and delinquency. Feminism is a program for increasing the number of such unsocialized males—whose antisocial behavior is then pointed to by the feminists as proving the need for more feminism.

Of course most whites will make more money than large numbers of disadvantaged minorities, as long as most of the former grow up in families headed by fathers, where the members of the family dine together at a regular hour and enjoy stimulating conversation at the dinner table, where the father helps his children with their homework after dinner, and where there are interesting magazines and shelves filled with good books—and as long as many of the latter grow up in households headed by women, where children perceive evidence on every side that to be responsible is to be female, and where the father's role as provider is usurped by a parasitic and wasteful welfare bureaucracy that tells large numbers of men that they are superfluous and can best serve their families by abandoning them.

Such men now have an additional burden placed upon them —an affirmative action bureaucracy that tells employers that they can fill two quotas by giving employment and promotion preference to minority women, thus further displacing minority men from their role as providers.

What of the effects of affirmative action on higher education? It is working to politicize our colleges and universities in unprecedented ways, ways that are discriminatory, racist, sexist, illegal, unprincipled, costly, and divisive. A decade ago, the following pronouncements by college and university administrators would have been unthinkable:

> Sacramento State College is currently engaged in an Affirmative Action Program, the goal of which is to recruit, hire, and promote ethnic and women candidates until they comprise the same proportion of the faculty as they do of the general population. (Roche, *The Balancing Act,* p. 28.)

> An announcement from San Francisco State College of October 8, 1971, of an "affirmative action plan" approved by HEW, calls for "an employee

balance which in ethnic and male/female groups approximates that of the general population of the Bay Area from which we recruit. What this means is that we have shifted from the idea of equal opportunity in employment to a deliberate effort to seek out qualified and qualifiable[10] people among ethnic minority groups and women to fill all jobs in our area. (N. Glazer, *Affirmative Discrimination*, p. 60.)

A letter in the *New York Times* of January 6, 1972, from some Cornell faculty members reports "that policy, as described in a letter from the President of the University to the deans and department chairmen, is 'the hiring of additional minority persons and females' even if, 'in many instances, it may be necessary to hire unqualified or marginally qualified persons.'" (*Loc. cit.*)

Sidney Hook quotes a letter to the president of the University of Arizona on March 31, 1971, from an HEW official who told him "Department heads should be advised that, in addition to the active recruitment of females, affirmative action requires that Government contractors consider other factors than mere technical qualifications." (*Loc. cit.*)

At one Ivy League university, representatives of the regional HEW demanded an explanation of why there were no women or minority students in the Graduate Department of Religious Studies. They were told that a reading knowledge of Hebrew and Greek was presupposed. Whereupon the representatives of HEW advised orally: "Then end those old fashioned programs that require irrelevant languages. And start up programs on relevant things which minority group students can study without learning languages." (*Loc. cit.*)

How long will the public continue to subsidize institutions of higher education that accept such arrogant dictation from ignoramuses who would have been flunked out of these same institutions had they been students in them twenty years ago?

> A January 12, 1973, memorandum from the Chairman of the English Department of College I of the University of Massachusetts, Boston, on faculty recruitment, reads, "At present, we are authorized, in accordance with the University's strong commitment to Affirmative Action recruitment, to interview only candidates from ethnic minorities." (*Loc. cit.*)

Glazer adds: "It has become common knowledge that minority faculty of any given level of achievement . . . would have to be paid more, if they were to be recruited." Such is the meaning of "Equal Opportunity" as we approach 1984 when, Orwell predicted, men will be saying, "War is peace."

> President Robben Fleming of the University of Michigan has already agreed to engage female professors for 139 of the next 148 vacancies on the faculty. (Roche, p. 58.)

> The faculty senate of SUNY at Buffalo has recommended that fifty percent of all new university appointments go to women or minority group members. (*Loc. cit.*)

The following announcements of job openings are collected by Roche, p. 6:

> The Department of Philosophy at the University of Washington is seeking qualified women and minority candidates for faculty positions at all levels beginning Fall Quarter, 1973.

> We desire to appoint a Black or Chicano, preferably female. . . .

> Dear Sir: The Department of Economics at Chico State is now just entering the job market actively to recruit economists for the next academic year. . . .

107

Chico State College is also an affirmative action institution with respect to both American minority groups and women. Our doctoral requirements for faculty will be waived for candidates who qualify under the affirmative action criteria.

Dear Colleague: Claremont Men's College has a vacancy in its . . . Department as a result of retirement. We desire to appoint a black or Chicano, preferably female. . . .

I should very much appreciate it if you could indicate which of your 1972 candidates are either Negro or Mexican American.

Dear . . .: We are looking for females . . . and members of minority groups. As you know, Northwestern along with a lot of other universities is under some pressure . . . to hire women, Chicanos, etc.

Your prompt response to my letter of May 12 with four candidates, all of whom seem qualified for our vacancy, is greatly appreciated. Since there is no indication that any of them belong to one of the minority groups listed, I will be unable to contact them. . . .

Dear Mr. . . .: All unfilled positions in the university must be filled by females or blacks. Since I have no information regarding your racial identification, it will be possible for me to contact you for a position only in the event you are black.

Administrators rushing to pacify the feminists, carpetbaggers, and other parasites who are swarming over us must know that this silliness has little support from the public which has to pay for it and which is becoming uneasily aware of the deteriorating value of a college degree. Our institutions of higher learning are more and more converting themselves into propaganda mills for feminism, homosexuality, radical politcs, and the destruction of the family:

108

While most Americans favor equal rights and opportunity, they overwhelmingly reject the use of conventional affirmative action and preferential treatment to achieve them. Moreover, the evidence is clear that the goals and tactics of the women's movement enjoy only marginal support among Americans of *both* sexes.

. . . .

Public opposition to so-called remedial action, busing and affirmative action is even more decisive. A recent Gallup Poll asked the following question: "Some people say that to make up for past discrimination, women and members of minority groups should be given preferential treatment in getting jobs and places in college. Others say that ability, as determined by test scores, should be the main consideration. Which point of view comes closest to how you feel about this matter?"

Americans rejected "preferential treatment" by a margin of more than 8 to 1. In fact, only 11% of women and 27% of nonwhites endorsed preferential treatment.

. . . .

In a national poll taken in 1976 for the Washington Post and the Harvard Center for International Affairs, the public was asked to choose between these positions: "Quotas in job hiring should be used to increase the number of women in good jobs" or "Job hiring should be based strictly on merit." 79% of the females and 82% of the males backed "merit," less than 20% of each sex favored quotas.[11]

Administrators and bureaucrats of course know of the public opposition to quotas, of their illegality, and of the opposition to them expressed repeatedly by the framers of the 1964 Civil Rights legislation which these administrators and bureaucrats profess to be implementing by the application of these quotas. Their method of living with these facts is to denounce quotas while employing them, insisting that they are not quotas but "goals and timetables"—an evasion as pitiable as that of the California legislators who professed to reform that state's wretched divorce laws by renaming divorce "dissolution of marriage" and by renaming alimony "spousal support." Or as pitiable as the following argument made in the Bakke case by Archibald Cox, the former Watergate prosecutor:

> The tall, crew-cut Cox, addressing the justices [of the Supreme Court] from behind the lectern much like [sic] he might a class on constitutional law, denied that the UC program imposed "quotas"—at least in the sense that quotas have been used in the past to limit the number of Jews admitted to professional schools.
>
> "But the Davis program did put a limit on the number of white students, did it not?" asked Justice Potter Stewart.
>
> "Yes," Cox answered, "but it was not pointing a finger at any group which had been marked as inferior in any sense. . . . It was not stigmatizing in the sense that the old quota against Jews was stigmatizing."[12]

The old quota against Jews was not stigmatizing at all, of course. It was imposed not because Jews were incapable of succeeding in fair competition but because it was presumed that in fair competition Jews would be too successful and would therefore displace less qualified non-Jews. Cox's assertion that nobody was stigmatized in the Bakke case, when UC Davis excluded Bakke in order to admit members of minority groups less qualified than Bakke, is as false as his assertion that there was no quota involved. Those who, with bureaucratic help, crowded Bakke out will carry the stigma of being quota-duffers for the rest of their lives.

Affirmative action might conceivably propel us into a new Reconstruction Era, this one nationwide rather than confined to the South. We might, before it is too late, learn some of the lessons of that first era and of the right-wing reaction that followed it. Those who refuse to take seriously the possibility of such a reaction have not read Rabbi Meir Kahane's book *Time to Go Home,* and they are choosing to ignore some important and increasingly audible signals.

> Listen to the radio talk shows that have given haters the opportunity to vent their feelings on the air to listening millions and the anonymity to screw up their courage to begin. One listens, and catches for an instant a brief look at the hell that looms ahead, a momentary glance into the ugly, sordid, soul of the hater.[13]

According to Tristram Coffin's *Washington Spectator,* 15 November 1977:

> Like the fabled Phoenix rising from the ashes of the past, an aggressive right wing is the most startling phenomenon of American politics today.
>
> . . . .
>
> The right would resurrect the old House Committee on Un-American Activities, which, *Congressional Insight* reports, "earned a reputation as a witch-hunting panel that used innuendo and guilt-by-association to intimidate people with left-of-center causes." The move to revive HUAC has 150 sponsors, and an omen of its use is in the *Congressional Record* inserts by its chief backer, Rep. Larry McDonald (D-Ga.). These are lengthy attacks upon liberals, radicals, the media and even fellow members of Congress.
>
> . . . .
>
> A political round-up in the Knight-Ridder newspapers reports: "In legislative battles in Congress, in political fund-raising, in mobilizing support on controversial issues throughout the country, in winning key off-year elections, and in sheer intellectual energy and talent, the 'New Right' has overwhelmed the traditional Republican establishment."
>
> . . . .

The *Manchester Guardian* notes: "In W. Germany, the former Chancellor has written to the Bonn government pointing out growing and violent activity by West German neo-Nazis. The recent rally of European Nazis in Flanders outraged Belgian public opinion. . . . In Italy court cases are proceeding against Italian fascists charged with terrorist outrages."

According to *Extra*, January 1978:

> The Ku Klux Klan in Pasadena, Texas, is sponsoring what might be called "Dial-a-Tirade" recorded telephone messages, advocating everything from the extermination of gays to the ambush killing of liberal judges. A recent message warned of the dangers of gun control, urging callers to think about "shooting" anyone from the government who comes around to collect guns if gun control laws are ever enacted. The KKK tells callers it would be "unwise" to shoot an antigun judge in the courtroom. "Use your head," it advises, pointing out that judges are more vulnerable to attack in their homes at night, or while on the way home.

The danger of such a movement is of course exacerbated by the outrageous fees asked by the legal profession, fees that virtually deny access to the courts to any save the government bureaucracies and rich.

Young people may be attracted, as indicated in the following from the *Los Angeles Times* of 4 August 1977:

> There is evidence of renewed Nazi recruitment on high school and college campuses, particularly where there are racial problems. In Seattle, the 24-year-old son of a federal judge is trying to establish a unit at the University of Washington.
>
> Prisons also may be the focus of new Nazi membership drives.

. . . .

Others are concerned that the movement is being orchestrated from a central source or that "outside money"—possibly from the Middle East or Europe—is being pumped into its treasury.

. . . .

The Midwest appears to be the prime future target, but no one is ignoring the possibility of Los Angeles as fertile area for Nazi racism when schools are integrated.

. . . .

"All these groups have been dead for years," he says, "and suddenly they're active as hell. Too many things are going on at once, and it isn't by accident.

"Something is happening. Something is stirring. Mergers. Coalition. Movement."

. . . .

Probably the most active group in the L.A. area is the National Socialist League, the gay Nazis. . . . (T)here's a whole new cadre of ex-Nazis around who are smart enough not to wear swastikas. They join the Klan now or create churches.

The unifying power of homosexuality in military societies is well known.[14]

Those like President Carter who are concerned about civil rights in other countries might wish to ponder what thoughts must be generated in the mind of a white Afrikaaner, for example, as he contemplates the spectacle of affirmative action in America. Might he not think something such as the following: "A few years ago the Americans were talking loudly about equal opportunity—of employing and promoting people on the basis of merit alone. Now they have abandoned the idea of equal opportunity and replaced it by its opposite—discrimination against white males. If this can happen in America where whites are a majority, what would happen in South Africa where blacks are a majority? If whites allowed blacks equal opportunity, would blacks allow whites equal opportunity when they had the power to deny it? Not likely.

We had best remain in control of things." Those who decry the absence of equal opportunity in South Africa and at the same time support affirmative action in America might profitably consider whether they are providing the rationale for such an argument.

Other right-wing movements are becoming visible. The following is a Reuters dispatch printed in the *Los Angeles Times*, 11 June 1975:

> BUENOS AIRES—A new nationalist movement sworn to combat Marxism and Zionism has emerged in Argentina with a recruiting slogan, "The best enemy is a dead enemy."
>
> Foundation of the movement, named Caudillo (Strongman), coincides with an increasingly violent backlash against the left throughout the country.
>
> It has alarmed Argentina's large Jewish community whose members say they have detected signs of what could be a fresh wave of anti-Semitism here.
>
> . . . .
>
> "If one of us falls, the enemy's total destruction would not be enough to avenge his death. . . . We will not destroy buildings, windows and people without cause." But if there is a cause, nothing will be left standing, the posters said.
>
> More than 100 people a day have flocked to the recruiting centers, the Caudillo spokesman said. They were being organized into "command groups" for political training.
>
> . . . .
>
> Slogans and symbols on the posters are reminiscent of Hitler's Nazi Party. . . . Caudillo admits that it is based in part on European Fascist ideology.
>
> Members of Argentina's 500,000 strong Jewish community say they view the appearance of Caudillo and other recent events with concern.
>
> . . . .

Right-wing death threats have been made against a number of Jewish personalities, including film director Sergio Renan. And there were unconfirmed reports that a right-wing terror squad, the Tacuara, which operated here in the 1960s, beating up Jews, was re-forming.

Two things would be needful to generate a right-wing revulsion: economic crisis and a grievance. These existed in the South during the era of the Ku Klux Klan and in Germany during the rise of Hitler. A very large number of economists are telling us that the economic crisis is on the way; and affirmative action is supplying a grievance to the most powerful group of American citizens—white males—by assuring them that they will not be allowed to be rewarded for their merit and achievement. So far, since the times are still relatively affluent, such injustice seems to be generating little in the way of reaction, and bureaucrats appear to presume that feminist clamors require more attention than the claim for simple justice by the one group that is unquestionably the victim of discrimination, white males.

Some of our universities (following the precedent of the Nürnberg Laws and the social legislation of the Soviet Union and the Union of South Africa) employ census reporters to make ethnic identifications of employees and prospective employees (usually without their knowledge) and to report on their skin color in order to determine who should be employed, promoted, or dismissed. Public school systems have found it necessary to classify students and teachers by race—often in defiance of state laws—to determine who should be removed from their neighborhoods.

It is becoming common to make large profits via affirmative action programs without having a viable case at all. The following news story describes one of the smaller settlements:

COLLEGE AGREES TO PAY
$80,000 IN BIAS CASE
Without admitting guilt, Contra Costa College has agreed to pay $80,000 to settle a suit which charged that the college discriminated against Mexican-Americans.

> A statement signed by attorneys for both sides said the settlement was "*to avoid the burden, the expense and the uncertainty of continued litigation.*"
>
> A 1973 suit alleged that Joseph Crofts was dismissed from a counseling position and Luis Sosa was denied a college job because of their heritage.
>
> In a consent decree signed in federal court, the college agreed to pay Crofts $40,000 and Sosa $13,000. A sum of $27,000 was to be paid to the Mexican-American Legal Defense and Education Fund. The decree also called for efforts to improve opportunities for "Spanish-heritage persons" at the college. (*Los Angeles Times,* 20 November 1977; emphasis added.)

The qualifications of the people named were never an issue. All that was needed was to hire a law firm (at the public's expense) and raise a clamor.

ITT was shaken down for $125 million in wage adjustments and back pay to women and minority men; and there have been similar chousings of Merrill Lynch, Pierce, Fenner and Smith; NBC; and the *Reader's Digest* (*Newsweek,* 28 November 1977). All of the cost of this inanity is of course passed on to taxpayers and consumers.

"There is no requirement in Title VII," wrote Senators Joseph Clark and Clifford Case at the time when the Civil Rights bill was being debated in 1964, "that an employer maintain a racial balance in his work force. On the contrary, any deliberate attempt to maintain a racial balance,[15] whatever such balance may be, would involve a violation of Title VII because maintaining such a balance would require an employer to hire or refuse to hire on the basis of race."[16] In less than a decade we moved from this to "We desire to appoint a Black or a Chicano, preferably female."

If there are to be quotas, should there not be religious as well as racial and sexual ones? It is notorious that Jews are overrepresented on university faculties, as they are in *Who's Who* and in the awarding of Nobel Prizes, whereas Baptists, Catholics, and Jehovah's Witnesses are just as conspicuously underrepresented in these favored groups. The Nobel

116

Prize Committee, in particular, must be not only sexist and racist (how many women are awarded prizes? how many are awarded to Ugandans or Haitians or to the Swedes' own oppressed Laplanders?) but also bigoted religiously. According to Joseph McCabe's *Rationalist Encyclopedia,*

> Of the prizewinners whose position in regard to religion is ascertainable, about sixty are included in this work, while fewer than twenty have declared themselves members of any of the Churches of Europe or America, and not more than three out of more than 200 are claimed in the voluminous *Catholic Encyclopedia!* Of about 150 recipients of the scientific prizes, the vast majority have never written or spoken on religion and we fall back upon Leuba's proof that 70% of American scientists (including teachers in institutions under sectarian influence) are atheists or agnostics, and, of the greater men, 84%. Of the minority of those prizewinners in science whose opinions are ascertainable, a score are declared Rationalists and are described in this work, while only four or five profess to be Christians (and are generally heterodox), and only one (Carrel) is a Catholic.

The most egregious part of the affirmative action program is its inclusion of onomastic criteria along with sexual and racial, which is to say its absurd pretense that Americans have been discriminated against—and therefore require bureaucratic favors—because they have Spanish surnames. Sacramento and San Francisco State Universities have declared that it is their wish not only to have the same racial and sexual composition on their faculties as is found in the general population, but to have the same surname distribution as well. This would mean, among other things, reimposing something eliminated in quite recent academic history—quotas for Jews. But why, if we wish to discriminate against Jews, would we then discriminate in *favor* of Sephardic Jews, so many of whom have Spanish surnames like Mendez, Mendoza, Franco, Spinoza, de Leon, and Abrabanel? And why should the relatives of Prince Juan Carlos de Bourbon be entitled to special bureaucratic favors because they have a Spanish surname, while the relatives of the Mexican emperor Maximilian be denied these same favors because they bear the Germanic name of Hapsburg? If John Archibald Martin is not qualified for special favors, why then is Juan Raoul Martin, who has the same surname? Is a Portuguese named Pereira entitled to claim benefits on the ground that his surname is Spanish as well as Portuguese? In fact, why would it not be possible for anybody to place himself on the favored list by Hispanicizing his surname? A Peterson could translate his name to Perez or put the nobiliary particle *de* in front of it and claim to have a Spanish surname. It's perfectly legal.

Many bureaucrats and administrators have already committed themselves to the follies of affirmative action and know that if they now reverse themselves they will lose face. And yet the problems created by affirmative action will not go away—they will get worse. The deterioration of American colleges in the decade or more that they have been discriminating against ability and merit in order to fill quotas is a familiar topic of cynical conversation on the part of the public and the teaching profession itself. It is better to acknowledge now that affirmative action has been an error, rather than postpone the acknowledgment until a time when it will be even more embarrassing.

What lies at the bottom of the problem is whether groups have rights or whether individuals have rights. The Civil Rights Act of 1964 was clear about the nature of rights: it declared repeatedly that there shall be no discrimination on the basis of race, sex, national origin, or religion (Title II and VI), none "on account of his race, color, religion, sex, or national origin" (Title VII). And Title VII adds that "it shall not be an unlawful employment practice ... for an employer to give and act upon the results of any professionally developed ability test provided that such test, its administration or action upon the results is not designed, intended or used to discriminate because of race, color, religion, sex or national origin. . . . Nothing contained in this title shall be interpreted to require any employer ... to grant preferential treatment to any individual or to any group because of the race, color, religion, sex, or national origin of such individual or group on account of an imbalance which may exist with respect to the total number

118

or percentage of persons of any race, color, religion, sex, or national origin employed by any employer...." Senator Clark, one of the floor managers of the Civil Rights Bill, when asked whether the bill would not require employers to establish quotas (translation today: "goals and timetables") for nonwhites, replied that "quotas are themselves discriminatory." According to the late Hubert Humphrey, "The proponents of the bill have carefully stated on numerous occasions that Title VII does not require an employer to achieve any sort of racial balance in his work force by giving preferential treatment to any individual or group." Senator Williams declared that the bill would "specifically prohibit the Attorney General, or any agency of the government, from requiring employment to be on the basis of racial or religious quotas. Under the bill "an employer with only white employees could continue to have only the best qualified persons even if they were all white."

Compare now these explicit and reiterated assurances with the working policy of EEOC:

> The anti-preferential provisions (of Title VII) are a big zero, a nothing, a nullity. They don't mean anything at all to us.[17]

A big zero indeed. Compare the following from the *Los Angeles Times* of 24 May 1972:

> Acting Los Angeles Mayor Billy G. Mills Tuesday signed an ordinance under which construction industry contractors doing business with the city must agree to hire increasing numbers of minority workers during the next three years. . . .
>
> The ordinance, which Mills, a black, sponsored 18 months ago, provides that by 1975, at the latest, minorities will be hired *at least* in proportion to their percentage of the total population.
>
> Contractors unwilling or unable to meet the *nondiscrimination* requirement will not receive city contracts.
>
> A minority is defined in the ordinance as a Spanish-surnamed American, American Negro,

Oriental/Asian-American and American Indian.
(Emphasis added.)

What we are talking about is not just panhandling but
illegal panhandling and shakedowns. "By every standard of
simple equity," writes George Roche, "by the standards of
the American dream at its best, in the interest of all individuals, especially in the interests of the 'disadvantaged,'
and finally in the interest of society as a whole, we must
understand that the egalitarian dream now pursued by Affirmative Action programming on the campuses of America's
colleges and universities is undercutting the very structure
of the open society."[18]

What of quotas for homosexuals, who now, with increasing vociferousness, affect to represent themselves as victims of past discrimination and therefore as deserving
candidates for bureaucratic favors? One lesbian gives us
assurance that a demand for such a quota for her minority is
unlikely to be made "in the immediate future"; but, in fact, the
demand has already been made, though not (at the time of
writing) enacted into law. Former Congressman (now New
York Mayor) Edward I. Koch's bill H.R. 2998 requires employers to seek out and hire homosexuals on a quota basis.
Incredible but true.[19] It would be interesting, in any case, to
know how Mr. Koch would define a homosexual, in view of
Kinsey's famous chart (Sexual Behavior in the Human Male,
p. 638) indicating that while there are few exclusive homosexuals (Kinsey guessed 3-4 percent) considerable numbers
of people have had some homosexual experiences. And what
of the claim made by some homosexual writers that everyone
is bisexual, so that there really is no such thing as a homosexual or heterosexual? Koch's proposed legislation, incidentally, would clearly violate the privacy of homosexuals
who chose to remain closeted.

Hear a lesbian named Francie Wyland, writing in the Los
Angeles Times of 3 July 1977:

> It is women's dependency on men . . . that prevents
> us lesbians from "coming out" and denies us free
> choice in every part of our lives.
> · · · · · · · · · · · · ·

120

But we're pushing hard for change. The lesbian
movement is emerging, millions strong. Just how
great our impact has been can be seen in backlash
crusades like the one Anita Bryant is waging
against us. Our response to her, and to others who
would deprive us and our children of a right to sexual choice, is the slogan that many of you have seen
on our placards today, "Lesbian women have
rights and so do our children!"[20]

"Once homosexuals receive official recognition as past
victims of illegitimate discrimination," writes Patrick
Buchanan, "the next step will be for affirmative action programs and quotas in hiring. . . . Homosexuality is not a civil
right. Its rise almost always is accompanied, as in the
Weimar Republic, with a decay of society and a collapse of its
basic cinder block, the family. . . . Homosexuality, then, is not
some civil right. In a healthy society, it will be contained,
segregated, controlled and stigmatized, carrying both a legal
and social sanction."[21]
Wyland continues:

Straight women in the International Wages for
Housework Campaign understand that the struggle for lesbian rights symbolizes a greater, common cause. What we all want is what they want:
the power to determine our own sexuality, our own
lives and the ability to live independent from
men—without paying the price of poverty, isola-
tion, overwork and forced childlessness.

This price can, thanks to bureaucratic machinery which
homosexuals can manipulate, be passed on to men to whom
they owe no reciprocal services.
Wyland again:

Last week, at the International Women's Year Conference at the University of Southern California,
straight and lesbian women passed the following
resolution, to be taken to the National Women's
Conference in Houston this fall:

121

Whereas our poverty and social pressure force too many lesbian women to choose between coming out as lesbians, and having and keeping our children, be it resolved that we demand wages for housework from the government for all women so that we have the power to freely choose whether or not to be lesbian, and whether or not to have children; and be it resolved that we support our children's fight for their own right to sexual choice.

The fight that the children are waging is not further identified; but Ms. Wyland's own struggle is clear enough: she and *her* children are to have a choice about their "sexual orientation"; but this is possible only if lesbians are subsidized by the government, and that is possible only if the government is subsidized by taxpayers, including the children's fathers, who are to have nothing to say about the socialization and education of their children—particularly if they wish to point their lifestyle in the direction of normal heterosexuality.

Wyland once again:

Wages for housework is an issue in which all women have a stake. But every women's issue is a lesbian issue, too, for every hardship on women— such as unpaid housework—is doubly oppressive for lesbians. No one—gay or straight—will be free until we women see in our hands the money we have earned by our labor.

Until lesbians are strong, all women are weak. Therefore we are fighting to destroy the conventional definition of what is "natural" and "feminine" for women.

What have we here? "Every hardship on women is doubly oppressive for lesbians." In other words, it is unfair that there should be advantages to women in marriage—that a husband (rather than a bureaucrat) should have something to offer a woman when he proposes marriage to her. "No one will be free until we women see in our hands the money *we* have earned." In other words, no one will be free until we women (Wyland is not concerned about men except that they be free to subsidize the arrangement she is proposing) see in our hands the money men have earned, which must be transferred from them to us by agencies of government. Women are not free if their husbands merely turn the paycheck over to their wives, since this leaves ex-wives and lesbians unsubsidized and, therefore, unfree.

Discrimination is notorious in the very regulatory agencies that are mandated to end discrimination. Roche wrote in 1974 that at EEOP there had been no fewer than 85 complaints about reverse discrimination in hiring on a quota basis.[22] This was almost 10 percent of the staff at that time. HEW flimflammer J. Stanley Pottinger has in his Orwellian fashion acknowledged the use of illegal quotas: "While HEW does not endorse quotas, I feel that HEW has no responsibility to object if quotas are used by universities on their own initiative." It goes without saying that he and his Merry Men have no intention of keeping their oath of office requiring them to enforce the law against quotas.

Quotas and the hiring of "qualifiable" (i.e., unqualified) candidates are of course incompatible with standards. "Neither minority nor female employees should be required to possess higher qualifications than those of the lowest qualified incumbent," reads the Higher Education Guidelines of the Department of Health, Education, and Welfare. In other words, it is illegal for an institution to improve itself or even to maintain already deteriorating standards. It requires little foresight to see what this means for higher education. Large numbers of qualified white males, realizing that their talents will be used as justification for discriminating against them, will seek other outlets for these talents. Large numbers of females and minorities, realizing that their sex or their race rather than their abilities will be rewarded, will crowd into the field of higher education, knowing that bureaucratic assistance will be a sufficient compensation for their scholarly shortcomings.

A word needs to be said about the formula that recurs continually in discussions of affirmative action—that it is required to overcome the effects of past discrimination against women and minorities. No person of integrity should affect to believe that American women as a class—the most

123

pampered humans, male or female, who ever lived—have suffered from discrimination. Their coddling and cosseting by American men is a constant source of merriment to foreigners, even to foreign feminists like Simone de Beauvoir. As for discrimination against minorities, the problem is basically that their disadvantages led to the discrimination rather than the reverse. What is required is not emphasis on grievances that facilitate panhandling, but a resolute attack on the disadvantages in question, whose removal will facilitate the entry of the minorities into the mainstream of society. Most of these disadvantages are associated with the parlous condition of so many minority families, a condition largely created by the displacement of many minority males by welfare. Another increasingly serious disadvantage is feminism. On this matter, Gilder is worth quoting at some length:

> The women's movement—particularly in its moderate manifestation—is the most important remaining organized enemy of black progress in America. It influentially opposes programs that are crucial to reestablishing the black male as the chief provider and supporter of the ghetto family—programs that might help black women in their beleaguered efforts to socialize the ghetto male.
>
> The chief requirement for giving upward mobility to any poor community is maintenance of a family and employment structure that affirms the male in his role as provider. If the male is the external prop of the family, he can venture into it without risk to his masculine confidence. One of the few successful movements for the socialization of truly indigent males in the black community—the Black Muslims—has learned this lesson—that the first step in restoring a poor community is to rectify the sexual imbalance bred by poverty. Because the males are clearly dominant in Muslim society, they can afford to submit to long-term patterns of female sexuality. They

identify with their children and hence with the community and its future.

. . . .

It is unfortunate that it is a movement of racial fanaticism that hit on this clear imperative of social regeneration. But as long as the rest of the society fails to recognize the need to reestablish the male, the government will continue to reinforce the matriarchy—thus ensuring continued anarchy and crime in the ghetto.

Andrew Billingsley has offered another example . . . of the effectiveness of special programs for *males*. In a study of "the sources of achievement" of leading black male professionals, Dr. Horace Mann Bond found that the crucial factors were (1) "a history of family literacy," (2) "a *father* with a determination of iron, an ambition for his children that is illimitable, and a disciplined mind that will exemplify and induce and foster good habits in children," (3) "a mother who shares these qualities with her husband," and (4) "a good school."[23]

One thing contributes more to success in society than all other things combined—motivation. Affirmative action destroys the motivation of white males by assuring them that their motivation, merit, and achievement will remain unrewarded. It destroys the motivation of women and disadvantaged minorities by assuring them that motivation, merit, and achievement are unnecessary for them, since they automatically qualify for society's rewards because of their sex, their race, their onomastic classification—or simply *because* they are unsuccessful. It provides two powerful disincentives for what it purports to encourage: if the "beneficiaries" of its programs do enter the mainstream of society, they lose the subsidy given to them for being unsuccessful and they must contribute to others less successful than themselves. What motive could they conceivably have for leaving the receiving end of the money pipeline and traveling to the input end to join Whitey?

Anything touched by an affirmative action bureaucracy becomes contaminated. If, under the sexist and racist principles of such bureaucracies, a status-conferring appointment should be given to a white male, the thought will occur to an impartial observer that this white male must have been exceptionally qualified, since he succeeded in spite of heavy discrimination against him. But if such an appointment is given to a female or a member of a minority, the thought will occur that the appointment may have had little to do with merit. Imagine someone considering treatment by one or another of two physicians, one black, the other white. Suppose he knew the two physicians had had the same training and experience and that they had graduated from the same medical school—and that that school had an affirmative action program that mandated lower standards for blacks than for whites. Which physician would he prefer to be treated by? The black physician would carry a stigma during his entire career because nobody could be sure whether he had been qualified on the basis of merit. The white physician would enjoy enhanced status from the knowledge that he had succeeded in the face of discrimination. Is it not clear that affirmative action must inevitably act to perpetuate and intensify racism rather than eliminate it?

Professor Thomas Sowell, the black economist previously cited, tells of his feelings on opening a letter in which he read, "Swarthmore College is actively looking for a black economist. . . ." This was Sowell's reply:

> (T)he phrase that came immediately to mind was one from a bygone era, when a very different kind of emotionalism was abroad, and a counsel facing Senator Joseph McCarthy said, "Sir, have you no shame?" What purpose is to be served by this sort of thing?
>
> . . . .
>
> *Many a self-respecting black scholar would never accept an offer like this,* even if he might otherwise enjoy teaching at Swarthmore. When Bill Allen was department chairman at UCLA he violently refused to hire anyone on the basis of ethnic representation—and thereby made it possible for me to come there a year later with my head held up. Your

approach tends to *make the job unattractive to any-one who regards himself as a scholar or a man,* and *thereby throws it open to opportunists.*

. . . .

(W)hat good is going to come from lower standards that will make "black" equivalent to "substandard" in the eyes of black and white students alike? Can you imagine that this is going to reduce racism? On the contrary, more and more thoughtful people are beginning to worry that the next generation will see an increasing amount of bigotry among those whites educated at some of the most liberal institutions, where this is the picture that is presented to them, however noble the rhetoric that accompanies it.

You and I both know that many of *these "special" recruiting efforts are not aimed at helping black faculty members or black or white students, but rather at hanging onto the school's federal money.* . . . (T)here are limits to what should be done to get [money], and particularly so for an institution with a proud tradition, at a time when the government itself is wavering and having second thoughts about this policy, and when just a little courage from a few men in "responsible" positions might make a difference.[24]

The principal reason for the large difference between the income and status of men and women has nothing to do with discrimination. It is the result of the greater motivation of men. A woman's importance is given to her at birth, built into her body. A man's importance must be earned—earned, in a civilized society, by work and achievement that enable him to function as an essential provider for his family. If women were economically independent of men, as the feminist and affirmative action programs wish to make them, men would have nothing to offer women. The male role would be destroyed, and society would become a vast ghettoized matriarchy in which women held the positions of responsibility and men sought to find a meaningful masculine role through violence, or sought to forget their predicament

127

through alcohol and drugs. A man with a family knows that the security and happiness of his family, and his ability to maintain a meaningful role within it, depend upon his performance and achievement. He knows that his sexual prospects and his hopes for a happy and civilized life depend upon his functioning as provider. A man considering marriage with a woman cares very little about how much status she has or how much money she makes. He does not intend to earn these things by marriage. Indeed, if his prospective wife were educated and capable of earning a comfortable income on her own, he would need to consider seriously the fact that educated women with indpendent incomes have the highest divorce rate of any group in society. If his contemplated wife were actually rich, his ardor could be greatly cooled by the thought that marrying her might cast him, or seem to cast him, in the role of a gigolo or a stud.

Gilder's *Sexual Suicide* and Goldberg's *The Inevitability of Patriarchy* explain why it is that the status of men is (and for the good of society should be) largely acquired by performance and achievement, whereas the status of women is (and for the good of society should be) largely acquired by having high-status fathers and husbands. The world's fastest auto racer is (at the time of writing) a woman named Shirley Muldowney. The status that she enjoys from being a champion must be a very mixed blessing. A male champion would be pursued by females desirous of having status conferred upon them; but a female champion is unlikely to be pursued by many males desirous of being known as the man belonging to the champ. Such men would feel like—and be thought by both men and women to be like—males who sought out and wanted to marry women who were taller and more muscular than themselves. (Not surprisingly, Ms. Muldowney is cordially resented by the male drivers.) Liberated feminist sociologists who imagine that they can alter the nature of male and female status by writing elementary textbooks in which women are astronauts and firemen while men mop floors and change diapers are engaged in the most preposterous exercise in futility since Pope Callixtus III excommunicated Halley's Comet.

Women, we are assured by the Swedish feminist Maj-Britt Sandlund, "should not be able to acquire social status and privileges automatically by virtue of their husbands' contributions to public life."[25] In other words, housewives and mothers should be treated with less respect than career women. A man should have no motive to acquire status in order to confer it upon his wife, since the woman can and should acquire it for herself (even though, it turns out, she needs help from the bureaucrats). But why, one must ask, would a man wish to have anything to do with a woman to whom he had nothing to offer, a woman who could brush him aside when she had a whim to do so (as half of American wives do), a woman belonging to the group with the highest divorce rate in our divorce-plagued society, a woman more likely to deprive him of his children and home and property and income than other women? Why should he not bestow his attentions instead upon a woman who would not resent, but be grateful for, his achievements and the status he could bestow?

A *woman* considering marriage is most properly concerned with the status of her prospective husband and with his ability to function as a reliable provider for her and for their offspring. Were she to fail to consider these things with the gravest care, she would be deemed vain and frivolous not only by her own sex but even by men.

"The value of an employee," writes Gilder,

> is far more determined by his motivation and career ambition than by his education and credentials. To most men, success at work is virtually a matter of life and death, for it determines his sexual possibilities and affirms his identity as a male in a socially affirmative way. . . . For a female employee the sexual constitution of money is much less important. Her sexual prospects are little affected by how much she makes. Thus even if the woman is a very dependable employee, a payment to her does not usually purchase as great a commitment as does a payment to a man.[26]

In his *Naked Nomads*, Gilder expressed the view that a man's need for a woman is greater than a woman's need for a man. What he ought to have said is that a man's psychosexual need is greater. But there is a complementary dependence on the woman's side: her economic need for a man. It is the complementariness of these needs that makes civilized society possible. It is the feminist-bureaucratic attempt to make women "independent" of men that is threatening to destroy this complementariness, and to destroy society along with it.

This complementariness, what Gilder calls the sexual constitution of society, is based upon the acceptance by both men and women of the fact that women are central to the human enterprise. Feminists have been insisting so stridently that "women are not inferior" that the point must be emphasized. Men really do have an inferiority complex. Few transvestites or transsexuals are women who wish to pretend they are men; nearly all are men who wish to pretend they are women.[27] One would feel very sorry for a woman who said of some book she had written or some project she had completed, "That's my baby"; but this is what a man says of what he deems his greatest accomplishment. Women who have not been confused by feminism know well that there are better ways of being creative than by writing books and devising projects. It is because they have this knowledge that they feel less compulsion to perform and achieve in areas where men must perform and achieve. It is because men also have this knowledge that "women and children first" is such a deep feeling in them. And it is well for the world that this is the way things are.[28] It is a grave threat to society that affirmative action is attempting to penalize rather than reward the greater motivation, aggression, and achievement of males. The health of society requires that male aggression shall be channeled into useful directions, and that when it is so channeled it shall be rewarded. What happens when society denies such reward is visible in the ghettos, where so many men continue to be displaced from the provider role by the welfare bureaucracy and where so much male aggression, in consequence, assumes antisocial form.

Millions of women *have* been confused by feminism into believing that the male world of achievement is the world that really matters and that the role of mother and wife is of secondary importance. Moreover, this error is being transmitted by increasing numbers of mothers to increasing numbers of daughters, of whom so many, thanks to our divorce arrangements, are growing up in fatherless homes. The health of society requires that women shall know, and know with deep conviction, that the role of wife and mother is central to society. Such internalized conviction depends upon girls knowing that they are attractive to men—something which, in a properly constituted society with properly constituted families, they learn from the first men in their lives, their fathers. Henry Biller[29] and many other investigators have shown that paternally deprived girls tend to be lacking in femininity and self-assurance in interpersonal relationships. They are more likely to be homosexual and to suffer from other psychic ills—which is to say (though these are not Biller's words) they tend to be feminist types.

The American way of solving social problems is to tax the honest yeomanry of the realm in order to subsidize paternalists in the government who use this subsidy—or what is left of it after they have skimmed it—to confer benefactions upon those deemed to be in need of them. The most paternal and protective of these bureaucracies is the Bureau of Indian Affairs, founded in 1824. Its success in advancing the condition of American Indians is not conspicuous. Is there perhaps some connection between the bureau's paternalism and the stagnation of those it serves? There is no bureau of Jewish affairs; and one cannot but wonder whether there may be a connection between the benign neglect of the Jews and their conspicuous success in academe and elsewhere. In any case, the two most obvious advantages enjoyed by Jews, their patriarchal family structure and their tradition of learning, are not the kinds of advantages that can be conferred by bureaucracies which, in most cases, weaken patriarchal family structure by functioning as father substitutes.

More and more males are being phased out of civilized society. Sexual impotence is the commonest complaint at campus health centers across the country. Dr. Paul Popenoe informs us that homosexuality has reached epidemic proportions. Transvestism, transsexuality, alcohol, machismo, and violence are commonplace. The plight of males, described in such books as Karl Bednarik's *The Male in Crisis* and Alexander Mitscherlich's *Society without the Father*, is becoming nearly desperate. What are men to do?

131

The fact is that societies have never discovered any psychologically satisfactory and socially useful thing to do with a male other than to persuade him to take his meager assets—his greater aggression, his heavier musculature, and his probably superior ability in handling abstractions—[30] and to use them to earn an income that he can then offer to a woman, through whom, and through whom alone, he may participate in the biological future of the human race—in other words, to create a family.

It is of absolutely fundamental importance for any society which hopes to remain civilized that it shall induce its males to make this last choice. Yet there can be few societies that expend as much ingenuity in devising disincentives for it as ours does. Affirmative action programs are becoming the second most significant of these disincentives—second only to the divorce laws which confront males with the fact that there exists a one-hundred percent certainty that wives *can,* and a fifty percent probability that they *will,* deprive them of their children, their homes, and the entire set of motivations that make them useful members of society.

Another consideration. Most of the failures of society are men. The small number of women in the most desirable occupations is not more striking than the sparseness of women in the least desirable places in society. Feminists clamor to occupy fifty-one percent of the seats in Congress, to be fifty-one percent of our research pathologists, judges, and corporation executives. We may believe that they want real equality with men when they begin clamoring also to occupy fifty-one percent of the curbsides on skid row and fifty-one percent of the cells in our prisons. This, however, is not the kind of equality these elitist ladies have in mind.

If one wishes to determine whether women are discriminated against, the way to do so is not to inquire whether most high-status positions are occupied by males or females. It is to draw up a list of *all* the occupations in society, from the most desirable at the top to the least desirable at the bottom, and then to note whether the typical female occupations (housewife, nurse, children's librarian) fall above or below the median of the list in point of desirability. One would not need to seek long for the answer to that inquiry.

Feminists are in a double bind. They have taken over the

first two points of the Black Panthers' program—unknowingly, of course. Point number one of the program is a demand for freedom; point number two is a demand for a subsidy. But to be free is to be independent and to be subsidized is to be dependent, and it is impossible to be both. The feminists' expectation, and their demand, is that their subsidization shall not be at the hands of husbands motivated by love of their families to place "women and children first," but by judges, lawyers, bureaucrats, social workers, and politicians who can bring about this same subsidization (which costs them nothing) because they have in their hands the coercive power of the law and the machinery of taxation. With these they can compel males to provide for females (and their army of attendant parasites) even after the motive of love of family is replaced by the motive of fear of prison. Such is the program of feminism—and of the police state.

Notes

1. *Affirmative Action vs. Seniority*, pp. 3, 5.

2. *The Public Interest*, Winter 1976.

3. Pottinger, after briefly transferring his mischief-making to the Justice Department, has now retired from what is called government service. He now calls himself Stan Pottinger.

4. *Los Angeles Times*, 14 August 1976; emphasis added.

5. *Los Angeles Times*, 6 June 1978.

6. *Rutgers Law Review*, 1969; cited in Florence Howe, *Women and the Power to Change*, p. 29.

7. *Loc. cit.*

8. *Loc. cit.*

9. Gilder, *Sexual Suicide*, p. 6.

10. "Qualifiable" means, of course, unqualified.

11. Seymour Martin Lipsett and William Schneider, *Los Angeles Times*, 31 July 1977. Another poll cited in the *Times* of 21 November 1977 recorded similar results.

12. *Los Angeles Times*, 13 October 1977.

13. Kahane, p. 36.

14. "It is this tendency to infantilism, rather than any

social censure of homosexuals, which is the reason why homosexual relationships are nearly always temporary and casual. Their basically autistic character permits no deepening or broadening of emotional relations; on the contrary, these relations tend to be impoverished and to atrophy. Homosexuality is fundamentally antisocial. It can achieve social value only in purely military societies, as in Sparta, a state keyed to fighting and war. Only in such a culture can homosexuality become institutionally anchored. . . ." (Karl Bednarik, *The Male in Crisis,* p. 86.)

15. This maintenance of a racial balance is precisely the intention of the administrations at San Francisco State College and Sacramento State College, quoted above.

16. *St. Louis Globe-Dispatch,* 22 April 1976.

17. Cited by Glazer, p. 53.

18. George Roche, *The Balancing Act.* LaSalle, Ill., Open Court Publishing, 1974, p. 74.

19. *The Anita Bryant Story,* p. 101.

20. The reference to "our children" and their "rights" is worth careful attention. Unlike the homosexual agitprop that ridicules the idea of homosexuality being "catchy," Wyland appears to believe that if the children of homosexuals are socialized to be straight and to think that family life is some kind of norm, then they are being deprived of their rights. Compare the title and subtitle of Jill Johnston's book *Lesbian Nation: The Feminist Solution* with its dedication: "This book is for my mother who should've been a lesbian and for my daughter in hopes she will be." As regards the "catchiness" of homosexuality, cf. the remark of a nursing supervisor who expelled two lesbian nursing students: "If you have a couple of them, pretty soon half the dorm will be lesbian."

With Wyland's remarks about the power of the emerging lesbian movement, compare the following from Gifford Gibson and Mary Jo Risher's *By Her Own Admission,* p. 35:

> As an eager pupil, Mary Jo was astounded. The infrastructure of the gay community was broader and more complex than she had ever imagined. It was more than a spiritual bond, it was real, a tangible, organized community. She was out, a lesbian

woman with limited practical experience but giddy
with anticipation.

21. *St. Louis Globe-Dispatch,* 7 June 1977. (It is not clear
what Buchanan means by "sanction.")

22. EEOP is "what many in Washington say is the most
mismanaged and overburdened Federal agency" (*Newsweek,*
16 January 1978).

Its "guidelines represent a qualified promise by
the commission that it will not cite employers for
violating the civil rights of *white men* who believe
themselves wronged by affirmative action hiring
programs. . . . In point of fact, [the commission] has
actually received very few such reverse discrimination cases relative to the tens of thousands of
complaints filed under Title VII," the chairman
said. "*Unfortunately,* there is a risk that even these
few cases will have a chilling effect on future
efforts by employers to take voluntary action."
[Translation: employers might get the idea that
white males have some rights too.] The key guide-
line is the commission's promise that it will dis-
miss *reverse* discrimination complaints in cases
in which the employer asserts that the action complained of was taken as a voluntary remedial program to meet fair employment standards of the
guidelines. [Translation: to discriminate against
white males.]
    The guidelines state also that:
    —Employers are obligated to comply with the
statute without awaiting the action of any govern-
mental agency. [Translation: they are obligated to
violate the statute in order to follow the guidelines.] (*Los Angeles Times,* 22 December 1977;
emphasis added.)

23. *Sexual Suicide,* pp. 128ff.
24. Quoted in Roche, pp. 22f. The emphasis is Sowell's.
25. Dahlstrom, *Changing Roles of Men and Women,* p. 219.
26. *Sexual Suicide,* p. 105.
27. Eight out of ten sex-change operations are from male to

female. (Walter Cronkite, CBS Evening News, 6 December 1977.)

28. The house-male Ashley Montagu ridicules the expression "*Man the boats. Women and children first,*" suggesting that it represents male manipulative psychology whose purpose is the exploitation of women. If your daughter is ever involved in a shipwreck, you may hope she finds herself surrounded by male chauvinists rather than by people like Professor Montagu, who not only believes chivalry is bogus but that the chief proof of the superiority of the female sex is provided by its greater longevity.

29. See the references given in Chapter IV, especially *Paternal Deprivation* and *Father Power*.

30. See Steven Goldberg's *The Inevitability of Patriarchy* for the evidence that males do possess this minor advantage, especially pp. 185ff.

VIII

Free Child Care

*We are establishing model institutions, din-
ing rooms and crèches, which will liberate
women from housework.*
                                    —Lenin

*It is no wonder if the better-placed workers'
families avoid child-care facilities.*
                                    —Trostky

*It is a system that guarantees, beyond doubt,
a steady quota of fresh neurotics for society
constantly to cope with but in the feminist
view the child should not, at any cost, interfere with its mother's "freedom."*
                        —Ferdinand Lundberg and
                              Marynia Farnham

ONE OF THE central demands of the feminists, probably the
one most stridently and repeatedly insisted upon, is for child
care centers, centers "free" to anyone who wishes to use
them. Those who think this a reasonable demand ought to
read the eleventh chapter of George Gilder's *Sexual Suicide*,
from which a number of the ideas in the present chapter are
taken.

Nothing, of course, is free: buildings, furniture, salaries,
utilities, lunches all cost money, and since the chief beneficiaries of a child care program are intended to be women, it
requires little ingenuity to figure out who are the intended
suppliers of the $20 billion annual largesse that Gilder esti-
mates "universal" day care will cost. (A more recent estimate
is $25 billion. Compare this with $6 billion for AFDC and $12
billion for the first six years of schooling.) "For women to
have full human identity and freedom," writes Betty Friedan,
"they must have economic independence. Breaking through

the barriers that had kept them from the jobs and professions rewarded by society was the first step, but it wasn't sufficient. It would be necessary to change the rules of the game, to restructure professions, marriage, the family, the home. Equality and human dignity are not possible for women if they are not able to earn money.... Society had to be restructured so that women . . . could make a human, responsible choice whether or not—and when—to have children and not be barred thereby from participating in society in their own right. This meant the right to birth control and safe abortion; the right to maternity leave and child care centers. . . . "[1]

They must have economic independence—in other words men must not have anything to offer to women which women cannot simply take for themselves. They must not be barred from participating in society—in other words, what wives and mothers do is not real participation, not comparable in importance to what men and elitist career women do. They are to have the right to maternity leave and to free child care centers—in other words, the costs of financing their maternal functions are to be borne by taxpayers rather than by husbands.

According to the Women's Survival Catalogue,[2] "The Day Care and Child Development Council of America is a national non-profit membership organization that has as its goal the development of a community-controlled, publicly supported child care system for all families and individuals who want it or need it. The Council feels that child care services are a family's fundamental right. . . ."

Economic independence, equality, and fundamental right, indeed. The ladies seem to suppose that a woman is "dependent," and therefore humiliated, if her husband assumes the costs of her children's care, but "independent" if these are assumed by employers and anonymous taxpayers. What the feminists mean by their fundamental right is other people's obligation to work to turn over $20 billion to the tax-eater, who, after helping himself to his fair share, can then remove his tax-eater's hat, put on his princess-rescuer's hat, which shows him to be a mellow fellow with the tender gender, and bestow upon the ladies economic independence, equality, and fundamental rights. Truly exemplary greatheartedness, unless perhaps the fact that it is other people's money he is

138

being magnanimous with somewhat moderates one's admiration.

The scheme is the familiar one described by William Graham Sumner a century ago: A and B put their heads together and decide what C shall be compelled to do for D. A and B are the good guys, the knights-errant, the Robin Hoods; D is the distressed damsel, the object of A's and B's noble compassion; C is the male chauvinist Sheriff of Nottingham whose enforced subsidization of A, B, and D is justified in terms of agitprop about his oppression and enslavement of poor, poor D. Sumner called C the "forgotten man" and, to facilitate his being forgotten as expeditiously as possible, A and B promptly transferred this epithet to the wretched and long-suffering D who, in consequence, no longer needed to pay any attention to wicked C but could instead play footsie with A and B.

What gets left out of this scenario is the motivation of C. Before he was cast into the role of the Sheriff of Nottingham, he functioned well enough because he was motivated. He worked at his craft so that he might return at the end of his day's labors to his hearthside, to his little ones, and to the shared joys of connubial bliss. What is now proposed by the bureaucratic Big Brothers and the feminist little sisters, whose benefactors and protectors the Big Brothers have appointed themselves to be, is that the oppressive C shall continue to work at his craft but with the motivation of the love of his family removed. Once the wife achieves the economic independence which Ms. Friedan covets for her, the husband loses his role.

But as Gilder says,

Nothing is so important to the sexual constitution as the creation and maintenance of families. And since the role of the male as principal provider is a crucial prop for the family, the society must support it one way or the other. Today, however, the burdens of childbearing no longer prevent women from performing the provider role; and if day care becomes widely available it will be possible for a matriarchal social pattern to emerge. Under such conditions, however, the men will inevitably bolt.

139

And this development, an entirely feasible one, would probably require the simultaneous emergence of a police state to supervise the undisciplined man and a child care state to manage the children. Thus will the costs of sexual job equality be passed on to the public in vastly increased taxes. The present sexual constitution is cheaper.[3]

It is no exaggeration to say that this prospect is staring us squarely in the face in consequence of the present condition of the family—which is being destroyed by the combined action of feminism and our divorce laws. Paradoxically, this very destruction of the family is itself urged as the reason why we need more feminism and more child care programs—which will in turn facilitate further family destruction. According to Congresswoman Shirley Chisholm, "The need for quality day-care programs will not go away; the changing nature of the American family assures us that."

Strangely enough, this attempt to slash day-care funds comes when the demand for services has escalated in response to changes in the nature and composition of American families. Television and literature may still cling to the idyllic version of the nuclear family in which the father goes into the world as a breadwinner, and the mother remains at home, happily tending children, but the contemporary reality is dramatically different.

In the past decade the number of American families in which no father is present has increased 10 times faster than the number of traditional two-parent families. This means that one out of every seven children in this country now lives in a household headed by a woman.[4] Many of these women have been forced onto the welfare roles.

Their dilemma is distressingly simple: Because this country lacks adequate public day-care facilities, a single mother must remain at home if her children are to receive proper attention. But if she does so, she cannot work and therefore requires welfare.[5]

140

According to Lawrence Fuchs, "by the end of the 1970s ... it is possible that most American preschool children will have working mothers."[6] And one may be sure that an increasing number of these mothers will be single. (Walter Cronkite informed us in a Fall 1976 broadcast that the illegitimacy rate in Washington, D.C. now exceeds 50 percent.)

The sociological problem has a political aspect, which is thus interpreted by the feminist Caroline Lund in her introduction to Trotsky's *Woman and the Family*: "The basic demands of the women's liberation movement certainly lead in the direction of socialism, by spreading the idea that the functions of the family (child care, cooking, laundry, cleaning, medical care, etc.) should be socialized, that is, provided free for everyone."[7]

According to the feminists Louise Gross and Phyllis MacEwan, the "care" provided by day centers ought to include indoctrination:

WHY WE MUST DEMAND SPACE AND MONEY AND NOT THE DAY CARE CENTERS THEMSELVES

. . . .

As radicals *we* must understand that *our* goals for children are in conflict with those of the institutions—corporations and universities—from whom we will be demanding day care services. This implies that when we make demands for day care they should be solely in terms of money and space. The corporations should have no control.[8] (Emphasis added.)

In other words, a minority of self-proclaimed radicals is to appoint itself to supervise the propaganda disseminated in day care centers and is to impose its views on the children who attend them, with the majority of the parents and the people who pay for the centers having nothing to say about the matter.

The IWY conference (federally funded, naturally) that met in Houston in November 1977 called upon the federal government to "assume a major role in directing and providing comprehensive, voluntary, flexible-hour, bias-free, non-

sexist, quality child care and developmental programs."[9]
And so if you wish to bring up your sons with the expectation
that they will be providers for their families, and to bring up
your daughters with the expectation that they will be
mothers and housewives, then you must pay for your child
care out of your own pocket. But if you wish to bring them up
believing that male and female roles are interchangeable and
that being homosexual is just as good as being heterosexual,
then you are privileged to pass the cost of child care on to old-
fashioned people who disagree with you.

Gross and MacEwan continue:

> It is well documented that attitudes toward work,
> race, sex (including male/female roles), and co-
> operation are being formed during the first five
> years of life. It follows that *as radicals,* concerned
> with developing a radical consciousness on these
> issues, *we* need to be seriously concerned with
> what happens inside the day care center. (Empha-
> sis added.)

Most feminists assume as a matter of course that such
centers will be, and should be, used for propaganda purposes, as they are in the USSR. According to Fuchs (p. 220),
"The Soviet government has always favored communal child
facilities where Communist ideals can be instilled into children." But he adds significantly, "Large numbers of Soviet
mothers do not take advantage of them. . . . Only about 10 percent of the Soviet children under age two and 20 percent between ages 3 and 7 are enrolled in nurseries or kinder-
gartens."

Gross and MacEwan demand a rejection of the ideology
which says "that women belong in the home."

> The primary reason for demanding day care is the
> liberation of women. While recognizing that day
> care is essential for women's liberation, the
> authors want the movement to further recognize
> that day care is essential for the liberation of chil-
> dren. Group child care, in contrast to the more
> isolating private home environment, has the poten-

142

tial of providing an environment in which children will have more opportunity to develop social sensitivity and responsibility, emotional autonomy and trust, and a wider range of intellectual interests.

Translated out of feminese this means the children are to receive ample doses of radical propaganda. Those who hold differing views need not be consulted.

Gross and MacEwan again:

Women, of course, will gain from a good day care program, but in the final analysis women's liberation depends on an entire transformation of society, not just one institution. However, that one institution, if radically structured, can help obtain that transformation.

In order to develop a radically structured day care program we must not allow any control to be in the hands of the universities and corporations. Our demand to these institutions for day care must be a demand solely for space and money. Control must rest with those who struggle for and use the center. (Emphasis added.)

And they go on to discuss how to develop "the day care center as a base for community political action."

"In a properly organized society," we are informed by Mlle. Simone de Beauvoir, "children would be largely taken in charge by the community and the mother cared for and helped. . . ." And yet the institutional care of children, like the institutional care of the old, is a scandal. "In one study in New York City, 80 percent of the known and inspected day-care centers were rated as inadequate."[10] "We are establishing model institutions," boasted Lenin shortly after the Revolution, "dining rooms and crèches, which will liberate women from housework . . . from their state of domestic slavery."[11] Yet Trotsky, who fully supported this program, admitted that "the existing child-care facilities, even in Moscow, Leningrad, and other centers, are not satisfactory as a general rule to the least fastidious demands. . . . It is no

143

wonder if the better-placed workers' families avoid child-care facilities." And he acknowledged that in any case "the number even of these 'bad orphan asylums' was insignificant" and that most mothers would continue to rear their own children.

The same shortage of qualified staff exists in the United States today: there are too few people to staff existing centers, and the ones who are employed are often unqualified.[12]

The situation at present is this: in a shrinking job market with rising unemployment, the government is telling mothers that they are unnecessary as housewives and child-rearers, but needed as contributors to the labor market. They will be assisted in entering and rising in this market by an affirmative action program and by tax-gatherers who will amerce males in order to make females the beneficiaries of preferential hiring policies and child care facilities. All this will enable them to take jobs away from the breadwinners who subsidize their preferential treatment.

Four groups will principally benefit from this policy: low-wage employers, who will have at their disposal regiments of cheap female labor released from the care of their children; bureaucrats who will earn their paychecks by engineering this shift of women from homes to the sites where their cheap labor is wanted; divorcées who can function without husbands by foisting their children onto the public's charge; and middle- and upper-class families who wish to have two incomes and who can do so by passing the cost of looking after their children on to families who believe that having a mother in the home is more important than having a Caribbean vacation. Poor women will gain nothing. Concerning existing federal day care centers for low-income families—centers costing some $700 million in 1972—Gilder writes that the mothers' jobs,

> in the 20 percent of cases where they actually materialize, almost never pay as much as the costs of the training and day care—which in turn are higher than the welfare payments. The mothers do drudgery; their children get institutional care, otherwise unnecessary; the politicians are acclaimed for "toughness"; and the taxpayer foots the bill. . . .

144

Universal day care would hurt the poor and the
family, while giving a multi-billion dollar impetus
to upper-class "women's liberation." . . . The
damage to the poor comes in several forms. The
jobs available to poor mothers are poor jobs, many
of them not even covered by the $3,960 minimum
wage. In pure financial terms, the women lose.
They give up welfare, which pays as much or more
if they have a large family, and they incur expenses
of their job in transportation and other costs. They
also submit their children to institutional care—
though most of the mothers can do better—and
submit themselves to low-wage drudgery.[13]

The society the feminists envision—in which women
would work and earn as much as men, in which their children
would receive "free" institutional care while they worked—
would be a society in which the principal male role in civilization, that of provider, would be destroyed. According to
Sheila Cronan: "Since marriage constitutes slavery for wom-
en, it is clear that the Women's Movement must concentrate
on attacking this institution. Freedom for women cannot be
won without the abolition of marriage. . . . All women must
join in this fight."[14] According to Kathie Sarachild: "When
male supremacy is completely eliminated, marriage, like the
state, will wither away."[15] The state is, of course, by no
means withering away. The burgeoning of its bureaucracies
and the ever-increasing rapaciousness of its tax-gatherers
is largely the result of the state adopting collectivist and
feminist goals.

According to Bonnie Kreps, "We must fight the institution-
alization of the oppression of women—especially the institution of marriage. . . . We must eradicate the sexual division on
which our society is based. Only then do men and women
have a hope of living together as human beings."[16]

A moment's reflection would convince such women that
the program they propose for us already exists in large areas
of our society—the ghettos and barrios of our cities—and
that in these areas the displacement of males as providers by
agencies of government has created a nightmarish
matriarchy and an army of displaced and unsocialized males
who have turned to booze, drugs, crime, violence, and

machismo in their pathetic search for their masculinity. Very different are the black bourgeoisie and the Black Muslims with their patriarchal families. (Radical chic social scientists make merry over the black bourgeoisie and their old-fashioned morality. As Gilder says, the one trouble with the black bourgeoisie is that there aren't enough of them.) Even in jail the Muslims are conspicuous for their good behavior:

> They are considered among the best of New Jersey's prison inmates—quiet, courteous to the guards and loath to fall into common jail vices of stealing, smuggling and homosexuality.
> "The Muslims don't give you any trouble. They are the coolest," said a prison spokesman. "They are well-dressed and well-behaved and keep the jail cool because of their discipline." [17]

It is hard to know whether the feminists would rather deprive children of their fathers or of their mothers. According to the *Syracuse Post-Standard* of 14 October 1976,

> Washington lawyer Ruth Weyand argued on behalf of women employees at the General Electric Co., who contend GE's refusal to provide insurance coverage for pregnancy is sex discrimination.
> GE's lawyer, Theophil C. Kammholz of Chicago, said the company had valid financial reasons for excluding pregnancy disability. He said 60 percent of women employees at GE fail to return to work after giving birth, and paying disability "would be nothing more than a form of severance pay."
> Kammholz also contended that women would receive over 300 percent more in benefits than men if 26 weeks of pregnancy disability, the same as afforded for covered illnesses, were awarded.
> Miss Weyand countered that GE's figures assumed women would stay away from work the full 26 weeks, whereas most whose pregnancies are normal can return after two weeks.

Aside from the question of why a woman should turn down

a twenty-four-week paid vacation, the notion that a two-week-old infant ought to be separated from its parents is appalling. Here is the opinion of three leading authorities on child custody concerning what parental deprivation of this sort would mean to a child:

> Continuity of relationships, surroundings, and environmental influence are essential for a child's normal development. Since they do not play the same role in later life, their importance is often underrated by the adult world.
>
> Physical, emotional, intellectual, social and moral growth does not happen without causing the child inevitable internal difficulties. The instability of all mental processes during the period of development needs to be offset by stability and uninterrupted support from external sources. Smooth growth is arrested or disrupted when upheavals and changes in the external world are added to the internal ones.
>
> Disruptions of continuity have different consequences for different ages:
>
> *In infancy,* from birth to approximately 18 months, any change in routine leads to food refusals, digestive upsets, sleeping difficulties, and crying. Such reactions occur even if the infant's care is divided merely between mother and baby-sitter. They are all the more massive *where the infant's day is divided between home and day care center. . . .*
>
> *For young children* under the age of 5 years, every disruption of continuity also affects those achievements which are rooted and developed in the intimate interchange with a stable parent figure. . . .[18]

The feminists who believe that children can get along without fathers—and without mothers commencing at the age of two weeks—need to be reminded of the judgment of Bronislaw Malinowski: "I shall prove to the best of my ability that marriage and the family always have been, are, and will remain the foundations of human society."[19] What is at stake here is Malinowski's Legitimacy Principle, which merits a second quotation: "No child should be brought into the world without a man—and one man at that—assuming the role of sociological father." The purpose of the Legitimacy Principle, the neglect of which has devastated the ghettos and barrios and is beginning to destroy the suburbs whose taxes support the ghettos and barrios, is to permit mothers to devote their full energies to the care of the young. It is not by reason of caprice or antifemale bias that the word bastard bears the double sense of fatherless child and unpleasant person. Take the Legitimacy Principle away and mark what discord follows:

> Facing economic hardship and a much higher problem of a broken home, brittle family relationships, and an absentee father, the mere struggle for existence becomes a major preoccupation, and the niceties of psychological developmant may become negligible or coarsened in the process. Growing up deprived also means growing up with little impulse control. Since the capacity to internalize one's impulses is a prerequisite for progress, handicaps mount. Fragmented families frequently germinate rage-filled children; and rage plus poor impulse control equals confrontation with the law.[20]

This is what lies at the end of the primrose path down which the feminists are leading us—a fatherless society generated by our divorce laws, by our alimony and child-support systems, by affirmative action, by free day care centers. The principal difference between the society of the ghettos and the society into which we are steering is that while the ghettos can continue existing by being parasitic upon the rest of society, the rest of society cannot do the same.

If, as the courts tell us, wives are entitled to the same benefits from the institution of divorce as from the institution of marriage,[21] the question must needs present itself to them, "Why should I mop this man's floors and cook his meals, when I can hire a lawyer (at his expense) and compel him to support me without my performing these tasks? He has nothing to *give* me if I can *take* what I want from him." But why, one must wonder, doesn't the question present itself to the minds of husbands and prospective husbands, "Why do we tolerate this outrageous arrangement?" Quite apart from its obvious injustice to individual men, is it not visibly destroying the family? A system that requires a husband to support an ex-wife but requires the ex-wife to perform no services in return is a system of involuntary servitude. It was workable when it operated only against limited numbers of men; it cannot work when it operates against tens of millions of them.

Attempting to reach the feminists and the parasitic ex-wives—or their lawyers, who earn legal fees by fawning upon them—is useless. What is required is a system of enlightened patriarchy—the abolition of alimony, child support, and the employment of children as hostages. We need not the removal of children from the home but the return of mothers to it, so that they can perform the most important function of society—the proper nurturing of children: nurturing them rather than pulling them from their beds at dawn, washing, clothing, force-feeding them, driving them through all kinds of weather and placing them in the hands of strangers—all for the purpose of liberating women from the role of motherhood so that they may pursue—or at least a handful of them may pursue—elitist careers.

NOTES

1. *New York Times Magazine,* 4 March 1973.
2. Page 99. Emphasis added.
3. *Harper's,* June 1973.
4. According to the *Los Angeles Times,* 7 July 1976, more than half of school-age children live in such homes.
5. *Los Angeles Times,* 14 April 1976.
6. Lawrence Fuchs, *Family Matters.* New York, Random House, 1972, p. 220.
7. *Ibid.,* p. 8.

8. In Adams and Briscoe, *Up Against the Wall, Mother,* p. 271.

9. *Human Events,* 3 December 1977.

10. Fuchs, p. 220.

11. *The Woman Question,* p. 53.

12. CF. the following from the *Los Angeles Times* of 7 December 1977:

> The Brown Administration (of the State of California), by its "shameful" and "chaotic" operation of state mental hospitals, has jeopardized up to $60 million in federal funds, a state investigative agency said Tuesday.
>
> In a scathing 30-page report, the Commission on California State Government Organization and Economy . . . said the present status of programs for the . . . mentally disabled was "inexcusable" and that a "shameful" chaos . . . permeates the state health delivery system.
>
> Despite repeated calls for corrective action throughout Brown's tenure as governor and in the last year of the Reagan administration, the commission said, the lack of responsible administrative action left it "with a sense of deep frustration bordering on despair."
>
> . . . .
>
> Failure to meet standards has already resulted in the state Health Department's Licensing and Certification Division refusing to license four state mental hospitals. . . .
>
> The unprecedented action by one division of the state Health Department against another prompted the federal government to discontinue federal aid amounting to $1.5 million monthly per hospital.
>
> . . . .
>
> (I)n Nov., 1977, four years after the issuance of a Senate committee report, and nearly two years after this commission's (first) report, most state hospitals face the imminent prospect of loss of licensure.

The commission said the state hospital system
was a "disgrace. . . . "

13. Gilder, *Sexual Suicide,* pp. 164, 167f.

14. *Radical Feminism,* p. 219. "All women" evidently includes those who disagree.

15. *The Newsletter,* vol. 1, no. 3, May 1, 1969.

16. *Radical Feminism,* p. 239.

17. *Los Angeles Times,* 25 November 1976.

18. Goldstein, Freud and Solnit, *Beyond the Best Interests
of the Child,* pp. 31, 33.

19. *Marriage, Past and Present,* p. 28.

20. Harvey Kaye, *Male Survival,* p. 117.

21. I have cited *Butler v. Butler,* Virginia Supreme Court,
9-2-76: "The rule applicable here requires a husband, within
his financial ability, to maintain his former wife in a manner
to which she was accustomed during the marriage."

IX

Götterdämmerung

*War can be a final refuge of uncertain male
identity.*
—G. J. Barker-Benfield

"THE MALE," WE are informed by Mademoiselle Simone de Beauvoir, in introducing her apologia for lesbianism, "the male inhabits a sensual world of sweetness, affection, gentleness, a feminine world."

It would be an interesting statistic, if it could be determined, to know how many hours of Mlle. de Beauvoir's life have been spent in operating a jackhammer, leaning over a drawing board, doing double-entry bookkeeping, plowing a field, or being instructed in close-order drill under the supervision of a sadistic noncommissioned officer.

One suspects not many. One suspects that Mlle. de Beauvior knows no more about the life of the average working stiff than the fine ladies of Marie Antoinette's court knew about the lives of the shepherdesses whose costumes and occupational title they affected to assume.

The world of sweetness, affection, and gentleness of which Mlle. de Beauvoir writes is a world made possible, for both men and women, by the labor of men, who provide the ecomonic base for it. And the program of the feminists is one to exclude men from the sensual world of sweetness, affec-

152

tion, and gentleness, while still requiring them to provide the economic base—via alimony, child support, and taxes.

I have on my desk, as I write, a 21-page booklet entitled *Revolution: Tomorrow Is Now,* published by the National Organization of Women. Its vocabulary is a semantic nightmare. On its first page alone there occur the following: law — states — rights — prohibitions — titles II, III, IV, VII — federal funding — rights — act — legislation — commissions — boards — appointive bodies — rights — commission — mandate — studies — rights — legislation — rights — rights — commission — study — reports — law — prohibition — prohibitions — state — laws — legislation — action policies — hiring practices — agencies — benefits — economic — task force — resolutions — task force on compliance — rights — agencies — caucus — rights — government — committee — hearings — federal enforcement — public programs — agencies — executive departments — programs — enforcement programs — procedures — enforcement — records — allocation of resources — conference — compliance task force — hearings — priority — rights — commission — program — mandate — jurisdiction — appropriations — policies — office of federal contract compliance — rules — regulations — require — federal contractors — report — affirmative action — plans — taxes — finance — contracts — enforcement act — amendments — enforcement authority — federal — state — demand — childcare facilities — standard — requirement to provide child care — affirmative action program — state — federal — county — municipal — law — program — demand — services — administration — department of commerce — program — federal programs — demand — department of labor — insist — federally required — committee — programs — documents.

What kind of psychic life must go on, what kind of dreams must occur at night, in the head of a feminist capable of crowding all this clangorous jargon onto a single page of prose—this endless succession of demands, of imperative exhortations, of rescripts directed to agencies of government, requiring them to mandate what these haughty feminists desire shall be mandated? Did the writer of this dreadful page ever experience the emotion of love, or have an assignation with a member of the opposite sex, or fondle an

153

infant, or visit a sick patient in the hospital, or make a contribution to a charitable cause, or shed a wistful tear?

One must not judge, but one must try to understand. Is not this grasping and clawing of the feminists to arrogate to themselves the wealth and power of government—is it not, when properly understood, an expression of their need for love? The thorn of the rose, we are informed by botanists, is a made-over bud, that should have brought new life, creativity, beauty, and fragrance into the world, but that has instead been turned into a dagger against it. The stinger of the bee, the most dreadful weapon in the world of insects, we are informed by entomologists, is a made-over ovipositor, likewise an organ designed to bring life into the world.

There is much to reflect upon in this association between thwarted love, thwarted creativity, thwarted femininity, and violence.[1] And there is much to reflect upon in the association between this thwarted femininity on the one hand and the increasing power of big government on the other—for, as the litany beginning on p. 153 indicates, it is to big government that the inadequate and unloved will turn in their distress. And big government, in order that its empire may be extended as widely as possible, does not look with disfavor upon the growing numbers of the weak and the inadequate who have been created by the destruction of the patriarchal family. Let us examine these relationships and see whether we can come up with a significant generalization.

Theodore Roszak, in an important, if egregious, essay entitled "The Hard and the Soft," has shown the existence of a connection between 19th-century feminism and the militarism that preceded World War I. Ours is the second era of feminism; the first extended from the mid-19th century to 1914. During that period, Roszak tells us, "the 'woman problem' was argued about, shouted about, agonized about endlessly. By the final decades of the century, it permeated everything." "No one who has studied the life of the West during the half-century before [World War I] has failed to recognize the astonishingly hard-boiled, war-prone style of the period." "Above all, one finds on all sides the ceaseless celebration of war and warriors, the ceaseless denigration of peace." And he goes on with a series of quotations from, and references to, writers and thinkers of the time. According to Theodore Roosevelt, "The nation that has trained itself to a cancer of unwarlike and isolated ease is bound, in the end, to go down before other nations which have not lost the manly and adventurous virtues.

According to General Homer Lea, "As manhood marks the height of physical vigor among mankind, so the militant successes of a nation mark the zenith of its physical greatness." The Irish revolutionary Patrick Pearse declared that "bloodshed is a cleansing and a sanctifying thing, and the nation which regards it as a final horror has lost its manhood."

According to the Spanish philosopher Juan Donoso-Cortes, "When a nation shows a civilized horror of war, it receives directly the punishment of its mistake. God changes its sex, despoils it of its common mark of virility, changes it into a feminine nation, and sends conquerors to ravish it of its honor."

Roszak goes on with other references to Nietzsche, Weininger, Bismarck, Cavour, Spencer, Sorel, Lenin, Kecheyev, Kipling, Von Treitschke, Carnegie, Bakunin, Cecil Rhodes, Houston Stewart Chamberlin, and Jack London, "bully boys and great predators one and all, for whom the world is a jungle, a battleground, a gladiatorial arena." And this attitude was not confined to intellectuals, but was found also in "newspapers, magazines, novels, dramas, scholarship, pamphlets . . . that emerged from the ranks of now forgotten feminists and antifeminists."

The pre-1914 period, he tells us,

> reads in the history books like one long drunken stag party where boys from every walk of life and every ideological persuasion goad one another on to ever more bizarre professions of toughness, daring and counterphobic mania—until at last the boasting turns suicidal and these would-be-supermen plunge the whole of Western society into the blood bath of world war. Compulsive masculinity is written all over the political style of the period.[2]

Very good. To this point Roszak's argument is unexceptionable. But now he goes on to establish that the sexual insecurity of Victorian males was at least in part generated by 19th-century feminism and was a major cause of the militaristic atmosphere which resulted in World War I—and then he draws the conclusion that we today need, of all things, more feminism. (The man is married to a feminist, and his essay was published in a feminist anthology, so his conclusion was predetermined.)

> Now it is obviously no mere coincidence that, at the turn of the century, this obsessive glorification of toughness should coincide with the quickening tempo of the women's rights movement as it comes down from the 1830s and 1840s. As the women struggled to haul themselves out from under, they inevitably set the entire superstructure of male supremacy rocking. No institution in the society could escape the reverberations—and so the men were forced to cling to their endangered prerogatives all the more desperately. More than any other issue of the time, the "woman problem" laid the knife-edge of anxiety against every man's most exposed nerve: his domestic supremacy. . . .
>
> Surely it is this crisis of the sexual stereotypes that accounts for much of that extraordinary craving for violence which gathers so ominously in the last few decades before the war. *Der Tag,* long anticipated and prepared, might even begin to look to many men like welcome relief: the chance at last for embattled manhood to prevail in the one arena it could yet claim wholly to itself.
>
> . . . .
>
> If women's liberation in its latest phase means integrating more women into positions of power and prestige within our existing social order, there can of course be no way to fault the movement by the conventional criteria of social justice. Full-scale integration means equality, and against the egalitarian demand there can be no argument—

least of all by those who occupy the position of privilege. . . .

Again, there is no disagreeing with de Beauvoir that all masculine privilege must be transformed into human right; that every personality be allowed to find its own destiny unburdened by the sexual stereotypes.[3]

Is it not evident that his conclusion is the exact opposite of the conclusion warranted by his evidence? In the same vein we are urged by feminist Caryl Rivers to believe that traditional sex roles are "vestigial organs":

In the post-industrial society, the old sex-roles are vestigial organs. When homo sapiens lived in close proximity—and mortal combat—with the rest of nature, there was good reason for the roles to be divided into man the hunter and woman the nurturer. Brawn was essential to survival.

The society we inhabit today may have more in common with the anthill than with the lair of the saber-toothed tiger.[4]

Anthill indeed, in which sterile females run things and males are useless drones and studs. No doubt this is the kind of society the feminists envision for the future—created by the "legislation," the "commissions," and the "task forces on compliance" cited at the beginning of this chapter. But will human males, for all their docility in the past, docility that the feminists might, with reason, suppose to be infinite, consent to be reduced to the status of drones, or will they instead react in the manner that Professor Roszak shows their grandfathers reacted—preferring that the world should be bathed in blood rather than that their masculinity should be threatened with such contempt as the feminists show for it? Feminism attacks masculinity at its core when it asserts that the traditional male role of provider is superfluous and that women are perfectly capable of providing for themselves and their children. A society in which women took over the male-provider role would be unviable: if a male is to have an

157

importance in the family and in society comparable to that of the female, he must compensate for his sexual inferiority by achievement in the realm of work. "Women," writes Gilder,

> take their sexual identity for granted and assume that except for some cultural peculiarity, men also might enjoy such sexual assurance. Women are puzzled by male unease, by men's continual attempts to prove their manhood or ritualistically affirm it. . . . Unlike femininity, relaxed masculinity is at bottom empty, a limp nullity. While the female body is full of internal potentiality, the male is internally barren. . . . Manhood at the most basic level can be validated and expressed only in action.
> . . . .
> If women become equal in terms of money and achievement, there is only one way equality between the sexes can be maintained in a modern society. Women must renounce all the larger procreative dimensions of their sexual impulse.
> As anyone can attest who has associated much with "liberationist" women, this is what they try to do.[5]

Feminist Jill Jakes assures us, and we may believe her—indeed we had better believe her—that the women's movement aims at nothing short of a revolution in the relations between men and women. Professor Rivers, as we have seen, thinks that those of us who imagine feminism will blow over and "things will soon return to 'normal' again . . . have little sense of the future," and thinks that homo sapiens no longer lives in "close proximity . . . with the rest of nature."

But mankind does live in proximity with the rest of nature and always must; and our sexuality is a part of this nature. And male sexuality can validate itself only by work and achievement. The psychopaths who increasingly plague and threaten us, the terrorists and hijackers, are mostly single males lacking the provider role.[6] They are men, says Gilder,

> incapable of loving others. But strangely enough, they have a great capacity for attracting followers of both sexes. Charles Manson and the Sym-

bionese Army's Daniel DeFreeze are extreme examples. . . .

The system of raw power, implicit violence, sexual magnetism, and the potency of leadership . . . rules among the unmarried, who are living in the present, without dependents or dependencies, without a stake in the past or future, without children. . . .

Modern society in its great complexity and interdependence is . . . gravely vulnerable to the antisocial male: the hijacker, the saboteur, the mugger, the bomber, the "revolutionary." The failure to discipline their male aggressions is deadly to the social order. Schools or prisons cannot do it alone in a democratic system. Across a whole society, only the complex of roles in the family and the male group can integrate men.

A single man, independent and fearless, can terrorize a whole community.

What is the prospect for us if the feminists continue on their triumphant way, destroying the male role, creating alliances with bureaucracies that function as father-substitutes? Will there be "nothing short of revolution in the relations between men and women," as Jill Jakes, Betty Friedan, Simone de Beauvoir, Gloria Steinem, and most of the feminists believe? An apocalyptic prospect, if we may believe the words of Malinowski quoted earlier: "If once we come to the point of doing away with the individual family as the pivotal element of our society, we should be faced with a social catastrophe compared with which the political upheaval of the French Revolution and the economic changes of Bolshevism are insignificant."

But is there not an alternative apocalypse that is more likely, that suggested by Professor Roszak, the prospect that males, threatened by such a revolution, such a deprivation of meaningfulness for them, would precipitate a catastrophe that would confirm their essentialness. *"Der Tag,"* as Roszak says, "might even begin to look to many men like welcome relief: the chance at last for embattled manhood to prevail in the one arena it could yet claim wholly to itself."[7]

Such a catastrophe in a world possessing weapons undreamed of in 1914 is hard to contemplate; but of one thing we may be sure—it would solve the problem of feminism. Then the Betty Friedans and Gloria Steinems of our day would do what their illustrious predecessor Mrs. Pankhurst did in August of 1914. This good woman dutifully and patriotically put her leaflets away in the drawers of her escritoire, placed her placards in the back of her closets, and issued forth into the streets to distribute white feathers to men of military age who were not wearing the uniform of their country's armed services. Whether with a pang and a throe one cannot say, but Mrs. Pankhurst did at least temporarily renounce her struggle for women's rights and took up instead the slogans "Your King and Country Need You" and "There's Something About a Soldier That Is Fine, Fine, Fine." And, oh yes, also "Morale Is a Woman's Job."

NOTES

1. The Bob Hope girlie shows that gingered up the troops during the Vietnam war were intended to maximize their destructiveness.

2. Roszak, *Masculine/Feminine*, New York, Harper and Row, Colophon Books, 1969, pp. 87ff.

3. *Ibid.*, p. 103.

4. *Los Angeles Times*, 14 November 1976.

5. *Sexual Suicide*, pp. 14ff.

6. On the increasing numbers of females involved in violence and terrorism, see Frederick Hacker, *Crusaders, Criminals, Crazies*, and Norman Hill, *The Violent Women*.

7. In this connection, more attention is due to the erosion of the male role in the military by the admission of women, a policy that must seriously erode the ethos of what must of necessity be a fighting organzation. Lawmakers willing to appropriate scores of billions of dollars for "national security" are willing to undermine this security in order that protesters carrying placards may be pacified and quotas may be filled.

X

The Fairyland File

IT IS ONE of the charms of women that they do not reason well. This gives us poor males a comforting and reassuring sense of superiority in a minor department of existence, something we very much need in view of women's formidable superiority in most other departments, including those which matter most, *Kinder, Kuche,* and *Kirche.*

But will future generations believe how balmy our age really was—that our feminists would publish a lesbian magazine entitled "Long Time Coming," that they would wear T-shirts bearing the legend "We Don't Need Balls to Play," that they would publish a bibliography in which female authors were alphabetized by their first names, lest they be supposed to be the property of their fathers or their husbands? That a feminist organization—tax supported, naturally—would offer a course of study in how to cast spells? That delegates to a federally funded International Woman's Year conference would demand that housewives and lesbians be paid $800 billion out of "profits from corporations and money within the government."[1] Will they believe that judges held it a maxim of law that women were entitled to the same benefits from divorce as from marriage? That it was an age in which the Governor of the state of California, educated by crafty Jesuits, signed into law a bill permitting doctors to perform abortions but requiring them to try to preserve the lives of the aborted fetuses—which is to say that it is all right to kill a fetus, but that in doing so one must attempt to preserve its life.

In working up my materials for the present book I have had to push my way through vast quantities of feminist literature, and in the process I have encountered ideas and arguments so crazy that I have been unable to place them in my usual file compartments and have had to create a special "Fairyland File" for them. My Fairyland File, among other things, is, for me, a kind of refuge from the world. When my usual dysphoria deepens into savage melancholia, when the four humors and thirty-two amino acids make wars, tumults, insurrections, and uproars in my enteric system, when, in short, I can no longer cope, I pour myself a glass of Chablis, take out the Fairyland File, settle into an overstuffed chair, and spend an hour reading this incredible stuff. I am now going to share a portion of this file with you, reader. Prepare yourself for a feast of unreason.

Here is a passage from a feminist with the befitting name of Warrior:

> If men are going to destroy the planet Earth and all its inhabitants with violence and wars, all men should be killed, to preserve the rest of humankind. . . . The qualities of man make him unfit for life today. And like all harmful factors his life should come to an end. . . . As long as man is in power he will never admit the necessity of his demise from the planet Earth for the achievement of a humane evolution. . . . The tyrannosaurus had to become extinct.
>
> Because of the dinosaurs' huge size and voracious appetite, other life forms were unable to develop and survive in its geological era. . . . After eating all other species it could use for food, it died of starvation. . . .
>
> . . . If females feel some compunctions about eliminating him entirely, Man preserves and zoos might prove a rational alternative.[2]

If you believe that parasites exploit their hosts, Gloria Steinem will set you straight:

> Men and women are, after all, physically comple-

mentary. When society stops encouraging men to be exploiters and women to be parasites, they may turn out to be more complementary in emotion as well.[3]

Here's one from Barbara Burris that recalls a recent West Coast kidnapping in which, thanks to a phone call, the kidnapper knew that the victim knew that the kidnapper *was* his kidnapper, but the kidnapper didn't know whether the victim knew that the *kidnapper* knew that the victim knew that the kidnapper was his kidnapper. It gets complicated:

> A black man meets a white woman on the street. He is oppressed because he's black and so need feel no guilt toward her. She feels guilty because she's white. But then the balance shifts as she realizes she's a woman and therefore oppressed and needn't feel guilt. But then he feels guilty because he's a male. Then she begins to feel guilty because she's middle class. Then he feels free of guilt because he's older and she's very young and oppressed. She feels oppressed as a youth and therefore doesn't feel guilty.[4]

Bettie Wysor provides an example of feminist scholarship:

> Having fled Egypt, the Jews were a people in exile in Canaan during the time of the giving of the laws of Sinai which constitute the Levitical text, and out of which ultimately grew the Ten Commandments, the Decalogue.[5]

From the *Los Angeles Times* of 21 April 1976:

> Employees whose continued employment is conditioned on submission to the sexual advances of their supervisors may sue their bosses for sex discrimination, a federal judge ruled here Tuesday. . . .
> "A finding of discrimination could be made where a female supervisor imposed the criteria

(sexual demands) upon only the male employees in her office," [U.S. District Judge Charles R.] Richey said.

"So could a finding of discrimination be made if the supervisor were a homosexual."

"However," he said, "sex discrimination probably could not be raised as an issue if the supervisor was bisexual and made demands on employees of each sex."

Barbara Burris:

The fact that each male petty colonialist has an individual interest in perpetuating the subjection of his individual territory, i.e., woman, makes the colonization of women more complete than that of any other group.[6]

And she then adds this, the cruelest part of all:

The colonial rule is more intense for females as we have no escape into a ghetto.

Helen Diner:

Female predominance among the Celts began in the astral sphere.[7]

Maj-Britt Sundland:

The present marriage law of Sweden, which came into force on 1 January 1921, is based on the principle of equality of man and woman. Marriages can be contracted by men who have attained the age of 21 and by women of at least 18. . . .

In the event of the husband being the only party earning a cash income, he is under an obligation to contribute not only toward the expenses of the household but also toward the individual requirements of his wife.[8]

Joan Leech:

> Some women fantasize about killing their mates. When the fantasy becomes a reality, it is time to seek help.[9]

Sheila Cronan:

> The marriage contract is . . . a farce created to give women the illusion that they are consenting to a mutually beneficial relationship when in fact they are signing themselves into slavery.[10]

Then this on the same page:

> Divorce is against the interests of women. Many of us have suspected this for some time because of the eagerness with which men have taken up the cause of divorce reform.

(By which she means making divorce easier.)

From the same writer:

> Freedom for women cannot be won without the abolition of marriage. . . .
> The marriage relationship is so physically and emotionally draining for women that we must extricate ourselves if for no other reason than to have the time and energy to devote ourselves to building a feminist revolution.
> The feminists have begun to work on the issue of marriage. It is only a beginning, however; all women must join us in this fight.[11]

And on the same page:

> (T)he high rate of remarriage among divorced persons shows that divorce is not evidence for the decline of marriage. . . . And the fact is that marriage rates have been on the increase.

So "freedom for women" excludes the freedom to do what Cronan shows most of them wish to do—get married. Feminist concern for the sufferings of married women, it turns out, comes from single women who have been mercifully spared, or who have happily removed themselves from the toils of connubial life. Their concern is that others should share their happiness.

Helen Diner again:

> Amazon babies never drank out of their mothers' breasts but sucked on the breasts of their totem mothers, the mares. Adult Amazons partook of a vitamin-enriched diet of mare's milk, honey, blood issuing forth from dying animals, raw meat of animals they had killed, and the marrow of reeds, gathered before the dew settled upon vegetation. They had no bread and ate no carbohydrates, even after agrarian nations began to pay tribute to them.[12]

Diner believes in Gorgons as well as Amazons:

> The tribe of the Gorgons later recuperated, grew in power, and was raided by an expedition under Perseus, much like the expedition of Theseus against the Thermodontines, which occurred many generations later. Perseus killed the Gorgon queen Medusa. It is hardly necessary to mention that names like Medusa and Myrine were Greek translations from the old Lybian.[13]

Diner's book *Mothers and Amazons* has to be seen to be believed. It's a whole Fairyland in itself.

From Phyllis Chesler:

> Perhaps the myth and reality of female (and male) sacrifice will cease when intrauterine biological reproduction ceases—or when the function is not assigned to one sex only.[14]

To which she appends the following in a footnote:

> *Perhaps* either of these events would occur more

166

quickly if women were to control the means of production and reproduction—in this case, the scientific investigation of contraception, extrauterine
birth, and uterus implantation, the economic
means to insure the eventual success of such research, and the political, legal and religious
authority to publicize and enforce the research
findings.

Reflect on the implications of the words "political, legal and
religious authority . . . to *enforce*." The woman has in mind a
bureaucracy of feminist meddlers and enforcers with authority to supervise human reproduction. Big Brother has a
sister.

Elizabeth Gould Davis:

Fatherhood and the idea of permanent mating were
very late comers in human history. So late, as a
matter of fact, is the idea of paternity that the word
for father does not even exist in the original Indo-
European language, as the philologist Roland Kent
points out. (Roland Kent, *Language and Philology*,
1963, p. 11.)
The *Encyclopaedia Britannica* (1964 edition)
says that where no word existed in the ancient
Indo-European for any concept or object, it may be
accepted as a truism that that concept or object
was unknown to the Indo-Europeans.[15]

A linguist who wrote what is here ascribed to Kent would
be fired from the poorest bible college in Texas. Had Davis
taken the trouble to look up the word *father* in her dictionary
she would have found that there are cognates for it in
Sanskrit, Greek, Latin, Armenian, Old Irish, Tocharian, and
Common Germanic, proving that it must have existed 5,000
years ago in Indo-European. The word is in fact *the* stock example used in dozens of textbooks to show that Indo-
European languages are related to one another. Davis might
as well have argued that because the Gothic word for mother
is unrelated to the common Indo-European word, the Indo-
Europeans had no concept of motherhood.

167

From Jill Johnston's *Lesbian Nation: The Feminist Solution*, a book dedicated to "my mother who should've been a lesbian. And for my daughter in hopes she will be":

> The early civilizations of the matriarchies surely emerged out of a once purer state in which the human species was unisexual—male and female combined in one self-perpetuating female body.[16]

There is much to reflect upon here: the equation of lesbian and feminist in her title; the intention expressed in her dedication that her daughter shall be socialized to be a lesbian; most of all Johnston's ignorance of what would until recently have been known to schoolchildren—that all species, genera, families, suborders, orders, classes and phyla except protozoa have two sexes. And she imagines herself competent to improve society by converting all women to lesbianism and that such a conversion would constitute a return of the human species to an earlier condition in which homo sapiens was unisexual. This sort of thing is taken with perfect seriousness by other feminists, three of whom laud her in comments quoted on the back cover.

More philosophical speculation from Ms. Johnston:

> Throughout the ancient world the ram became the symbol of patriarchy, just as the bull was that of matriarchy. It is a curious fact that according to astrology, the age of the bull, the Taurian Age, coincided historically with the last two thousand years of the gynarchates—4000 to 2000 B.C., while the Arian Age, the age of Aries, the ram, coincided with the age that immediately preceded the Christian era, the time of the patriarchal revolution. The Piscean Age, the age of the fish, embraced the Christian era, the two-thousand-year period from which we are just now emerging, and it is therefore appropriate that the fish became the symbol of Christianity.[17]

She looks forward to a period of tranquil progress under

matriarchal auspices, a period perhaps already prefigured by the cultures of Watts and Harlem:

The Aquarian Age, upon whose threshold we now stand, will be "inimical to man," as Macrobius prophesied in the early days of the Piscean Age. The "new morality" of the Aquarian youth of our day perhaps bespeaks a return to matriarchal mores too long suppressed by the materialistic patriarchal values that have prevailed for the past two thousand years in the Occidental world. The Aquarian Age of the next two thousand years will see an end to patriarchal Christianity and a return to goddess worship and to the peaceful social progress that distinguished the Taurian Age of four millennia ago.[18]

Elizabeth Gould Davis speculates about how men managed to take control of things away from women:

When recorded history begins we behold the finale of the long pageant of prehistory, the pageant of the great lost civilization that constituted the source of all these "wonderful coincidences." The curtain of written history rises on what seems to be the tragic last act of a protracted drama. On the stage, firmly entrenched on her ancient throne, appears woman, the heroine of the play. About her, her industrious subjects perform their age-old roles. Peace, Justice, Progress, Equality play their parts with a practiced perfection.

Off in the wings, however, we hear a faint rumbling—the rumbling of the discontented, the jealous complaints of the new men who are no longer satisfied with their secondary role in society. Led perhaps by the queen's consort, the rebellious males burst onstage, overturn the queen's throne, and take her captive. Her consort moves to center stage. He lifts his bloody sword over the heads of the courtiers. The queen's sub-

jects—Democracy, Peace, Justice and the rest—
flee the scene in disarray. And man, for the first
time in history, stands triumphant, dominating the
stage as the curtain falls.

The deterioration in the status of women went
hand in hand with the Dark Ages that followed this
patriarchal revolution as it moved slowly west-
ward from the Near East, reaching Western Europe
only in the fifth century of our era. In Europe and
the British Isles the last remnant of the great world
civilization, the Celts, maintained the tradition of
female supremacy until the fall of Rome, when
waves of Germanic barbarians sweeping down
from the northeastern forests met the surge of
Oriental Christianity as it spread upward from the
Mediterranean. Between these two millstones of
"masculinism" the Celts were finally crushed.[19]

The following, also from Davis, is intended in all seriousness:

The philological fact of one original language is
borne out in myth. The Bible (Genesis 2)[20] says
that "the whole earth was of one language and one
speech." Flavius Josephus says that "all creatures
had one language at that time" (Antiq., I, p. 9),
implying that the beasts also spoke. Louis Ginz-
berg says that language came down from above,
complete with an alphabet for writing. The Sum-
erians believed that language and all the arts of
civilization were bestowed upon them by a mysterious creature, half human and half fish, who
emerged from the sea and later returned to it. Looking at this legend, the distinguished exobiologist
and space physicist Carl Sagan suggests that this
sea creature may have been a visitor from space.[21]

Again:

Tiamat may have sailed down this broad river (the
Euphrates) from Anatolia or nearby Thrace in a

ship whose figurehead was the mermaidlike creature of the ancient legend, half fish, half human.[22]

Moving from history to science, Davis tells us:

Proof that the penis is a much later development than the female vulva is found in the evidence that the male himself was a late mutation from an original female creature.[23]

In other words, there is no proof. She continues:

For man is but an imperfect female. Geneticists and physiologists tell us that the Y chromosome that produces males is a deformed and broken X chromosome—the female chromosome. All women have two X chromosomes, while the male has one X derived from his mother and one Y from his father. It seems logical that this small and twisted Y chromosome is a genetic error—an accident of nature, and that originally there was only one sex—the female.[24]

Paraphrase: The human lung is a deformed and broken down air bladder, the human hand a broken down fin, human hair broken down scales. The large X chromosomes must be superior to the smaller Y chromosomes because they are bigger, just as early bicycles were superior to modern bicycles because they had bigger wheels. If women are superior to men because they have two X chromosomes, then children with Kleinefelter's syndrome must be superior to both men and women since they have three sex chromosomes.

One more scientific passage from Davis, and then I must leave her:

Since Venus is a new planet, as Immanuel Velikovsky theorized (Worlds in Collision) and as recent Venus probes seem to indicate, and had not yet appeared in the sky in Sumerian times, it is possible that the ninth planet was Hypotheticus, the lost planet that once orbited our sun just beyond the orbit of Mars and which is now represented by the thousands of planetoids or asteroids that pursue the same orbit today. . . . It is possible, as Velikovsky writes, that this hypothetical planet was destroyed by the *comet* Venus on its way to its present position and its metamorphosis into planethood. This comet may have struck earth, also, in its passage through space, thus causing the shifting of earth's axis that resulted in the world catastrophe of historical times. It could well have caused, too, the slowing down of the earth's rotation on its axis as well as of its revolution around the sun, thus accounting for the shortened day and shorter year of Sumerian, ancient Egyptian, and ancient Mexican (Toltec and Mayan) calendars.[25]

The house-male Konrad Kellen likewise looks forward to an era of matriarchal tranquility:

Presumably, in the coming decade, thanks to the more realistic and relaxed society resulting from a stronger feminine influence on all its aspects, infidelity will become even less of a disaster if found out than it already is.

It *is* a disaster—and it will become *even less of a disaster.* This is the way these matters are reasoned about by those who are "realistic and relaxed" by feminine influence. He continues:

The family as a unit would thereby be strengthened. . . . What we are likely to see in the different social and sexual climate of the 1980s, brought about by woman power, is that emotionally and terminologically the act of having sexual relations outside of marriage will be divested of the connotation of breaking faith, of betraying, cheating the one person most people are generally most attached to. It is a reasonable prediction that the terms "infidelity" and "adultery" will soon be designated by Webster as "archaic."

Ms. magazine in September 1975 tells of the judicial chivalry of one Judge Bentley Kassal of the Manhattan Superior Court. Seems there was a premed student by name Ethelyn Dyre Daniel who married a prelaw student by name Charles Morgan back in 1967 and helped him through law school by working in humble clerical capacities. So he becomes a $27,000 a year lawyer while she, poor thing, is capable of making only $10,000 with her typing and filing. An excellent reason, one might suppose, for remaining married and letting hubby pay her way through medical school, as per agreement. But no, Ethelyn wants a divorce, and with the benches loaded with princess-rescuers like Judge Kassal, who needs marriage? So Morgan gets stuck for alimony payments of $10,400 a year out of his $27,000 gross—not take-home—salary. "The money is hers on the condition that she complete her medical studies." Truly, as Ms. comments, a "remarkable" decision which breaks new ground in matrimonial law. "It was proved to me," says Kassal, "that Ethelyn Morgan had damned good potential to become a doctor, and I didn't see why she should be condemned to a life of frustration doing work she was overqualified for."

And Ethelyn? She's surprised but delighted. "When I began this case," she says, "I never knew it hadn't been done before. I kept thinking it's only fair."

The Ms. article is entitled "A Decree for a Degree," and is accompanied by a cute cartoon showing Judge Kassal placing a mortarboard on the woman's head while the poor husband's jaw drops and his hair stands on end. Very funny. Very gratifying to the sort of ladies who subscribe to Ms. Ethelyn supported the man because he was her husband and because it made economic sense for her to do so. And, there is no reason to doubt, he would have supported her through medical school because she was his wife and because he had promised to do so, and because it made excellent economic sense for him to to so. But the lady chose to become his ex-wife. And because of this choice a new set of rules becomes applicable. Previously the husband was stuck for alimony and child support because *he* had supported *his wife* in the past, and therefore *she* was deemed entitled to be maintained (consistent with the husband's ability to pay) in the style to which the husband had accustomed her during the marriage. Now *she* is entitled, in the view of Judge Bentley Kassal and his fellows on the bench, to be supported because *she* has supported *him*.

The constant factor in these arrangements is that the husband has no rights. Kassal could have done his bit for the stabilization of marriage and society by placing the son in the custody of the husband, thus seeing that the child was properly provided for and thus allowing the wife to pursue her career unencumbered.

"The money is hers on the condition that she complete her medical studies," says Kassal. But Kassal knows that the money is hers, period. Kassal knows that Morgan pays or Morgan goes to the pokey. No condition applies to Morgan and no condition applies to Ethelyn. There is no way in which Morgan could get his money back if Ethelyn fails to complete her studies. Ethelyn knows that if she does complete them she will lose $10,400 a year, and that the completion of her studies is therefore less attractive by that amount than their prolongation—by, say, going into a specialization or a part-time program. In other words, Kassal, who is so concerned for the "dammed good potential" of Ethelyn, has created a situation in which Morgan would be ahead if he quit his $27,000-a-year job as a lawyer and got a $10,000-a-year job as a shipping clerk—a situation in which he could not afford to marry again and start a second family, a situation in which few women would wish to marry *him,* a situation in which Ethelyn is motivated not to marry or to support herself. A situation destructive of the family.

Such is the service to society of the legal profession.

If it was proved to Kassal that Ethelyn had "damned good potential" and "I didn't see why she should be condemned to a life of frustration doing work she was overqualified for," then it was proved to Morgan that he was foolish to marry a liberated feminist-elitist with damned good potential, and that he should instead have married a dummy with damned poor potential, a dummy more likely to remain loyal to him.

174

If feminists were merely spinning tales about sailing from Thrace down the Euphrates River; about the Dark Ages being preceded by a period of matriarchy; about the Celts having matriarchal families; about language being brought to earth from outer space, or by half-human-half-fish from the sea; about talking animals; about the comet Venus changing into a planet; about women putting men into zoos; about hosts living off parasites; about female predominance in the astral sphere; about women needing help with their murderous fantasies *after* their murders; about freeing women by prohibiting them from being married; about Amazons and Gorgons; about creating an agency of government to supervise reproduction; about the concept of fatherhood being unknown to the Aryans; about early humans being unisexual; about the familial and historical differences between the Arian, Piscean, and Aquarian Ages; about the astronomical theories of Macrobius; about males being broken-down females; about the lost planet Hypotheticus; about strengthening the family by greater sexual promiscuity—if it were this sort of diverison the feminists were disporting themselves with, the Fairyland File would be merely amusing. But these women and their house-males are in deadly earnest in their attempts to restructure marriage and the family, to reassign sex roles, and to alter the socialization of children aimed at preparing them for life as responsible adults.

NOTES

1. *Human Events,* 3 December 1977.

2. Betsy Warrior, "Man As an Obsolete Life Form," in Sookie Stambler, *Women's Liberation: Blueprint for the Future.* New York, Ace Books, 1970, p. 45.

3. Quoted in Adelstein and Paval, *Women's Liberation.* New York, St. Martin's Press, 1972, p. 145.

4. Barbara Burris, "The Fourth World Manifesto," originally published in *Notes from the Third Year,* 1971; reprinted in *Radical Feminism,* ed. Anne Koedt et al. New York, Quadrangle, The New York Times Book Club, 1973, p. 333.

5. Bettie Wysor, *The Lesbian Myth*. New York, Random House, 1974, p. 31.

6. *Radical Feminism*, p. 336.

7. Helen Diner, *Mothers and Amazons*. New York, Julian Press, 1965 (originally published c. 1930), p. 250.

8. "The Status of Women in Sweden: Report to the United Nations," 1968. In Dahlstrom, *The Changing Roles of Men and Women*, p. 252.

9. Cited in *The Liberator*, December 1976.

10. Sheila Cronan, "Marriage," in *Notes from the Third Year*, reprinted in *Radical Feminism*, p. 218.

11. *Ibid.*, pp. 219f.

12. *Ibid.*, p. 127.

13. *Ibid.*, p. 135.

14. Phyllis Chesler, *Women and Madness*. New York, Doubleday, 1972, p. 31.

15. Elizabeth Gould Davis, *The First Sex*. New York, Penguin Books, 1972, p. 20.

16. Jill Johnston, *Lesbian Nation*, p. 256.

17. Johnston, *Lesbian Nation*, p. 265, quoted from Davis, *The First Sex*, p. 134.

18. Davis, p. 135.

19. Davis, p. 16. Cf. Goldberg, *The Inevitability of Patriarchy*. New York, William Morrow, 1973, p. 56: "I am bothering to discuss the presentations of works alleging the former existence of matriarchies not because they deserve discussion on their intellectual merit—they are uniformly inaccurate and incompetently done—but because they are occasionally invoked by laymen." He lists Davis' book as one of these.

20. Obviously an error; *Genesis 11* is meant.

21. *Ibid.*, p. 22.

22. *Ibid.*, p. 50.

23. *Ibid.*, p. 34.

24. *Ibid.*, p. 344.

25. Konrad Kellen, *The Coming Age of Woman Power*. Weyden, 1972, p. 149.

XI

The Homosexual Militants

Homosexuals form an international conspiracy, a comradeship which is stronger than that of the monastic orders and of freemasonry, which holds closer and throws a bond across all the walls of creed, state and class, which unites the most remote, the most foreign, in a fraternal league of offense and defense. . . . All rally together against the common enemy. Many of them look down on normal men as beings of another kind, insufficiently "differentiated."
— Maximilian Harden

IT HAS BEEN well said that the love of truth is the feeblest of human passions. If such love when directed towards indifferent and abstract matters is a feeble passion, it deserves to be asked, how intense a yearning for the truth is to be expected from those dealing with the most indomitable of human motivations—from, say, homosexuals writing on the subject of homosexuality, from authors who expect their books to be read largely by homosexuals, from politicians angling for the large, organized and deliverable bloc of homosexual votes. Answer: not too intense.

Such an absence of passion accounts for the curious state of affairs discoverable by anyone who does much reading in the area of homosexuality, where the literature is filled with illogic, tendentiousness, and misrepresentation, a literature much of which is written by closeted homosexuals using their research as propaganda, and much of which is palpably self-contradictory.

Let me illustrate. David Loovis, author of *Straight Answers About Homosexuality for Straight Readers*, tells his readers

177

(when it suits his purpose in one argument) that everyone is potentially straight *and* gay and that the notion of a homosexual having no choice about his sexual orientation is a depreciating idea which removes the responsibility for homosexuality from the homosexual's domain of choice, thus denying that he could have consciously chosen to be homosexual. However, when it serves the purpose of a different argument he tells his readers he has always been gay, and assures them that psychiatrists today have practically given up attempting to change homosexuals. Sometimes they have had a little success when the patient assists wholeheartedly, but usually such a patient has a major non-sexual motivation at work. He gives as an example a flamboyant young friend of his who went to a psychiatrist, turned straight, and got married. Bully for him, thought Loovis, if that was what he wanted. But years later he met him in a gay bar and asked him about his cure, not to mention his wife. He answered between dances that his family had threatened to cut him off financially if he was gay; but now his parents were dead, he had inherited their millions and finally he could be "himself." So much for psychiatry, says Loovis.[1]

So much for psychiatry—until it proves desirable, as it does elsewhere in Loovis's book, to appeal to the wisdom of the psychiatric profession. And so much for the poor wife of this flamboyant friend, who was fiscally useful but could be discarded when his parents died and he was free to resume his practice of cruising the gay bars. He could now be himself—which is to say he was homosexual by nature, not choice.

The homosexual Jesuit priest Father John J. O'Neill says the same—that sexuality is given and is unchangeable, and as homosexuals grow up they "become aware" of what their sexuality is. When they do, they need a role model of how to live out a good life as homosexuals.[2] California Assemblyman Art Agnos, angling for the homosexual vote, says the same and compares anti-gays who would like to solve the problems of gay people by making them heterosexuals to those who would solve the problems of racism by making everybody white. Agnos would have us believe there is no question of the choice of which Loovis speaks.[3]

Similar confusion hovers over the assertion that everyone is bisexual and that therefore there is nothing "natural" or biologically determined about either heterosexuality or homosexuality, an assertion commonly accompanied by references to the gay seagulls of Santa Barbara Island and to other alleged examples of homosexuality in animals.[4] From this the homosexual apologist will go on to reason that it is wrong to socialize children towards heterosexuality, marriage, and family living.[5] But the first proposition, that sexuality is given and unchangeable, is extremely dubious, while the second, that everyone is bisexual, leads to the opposite conclusion from that desired: if biology fails to make people heterosexual, if, as the homosexual Carl Wittman assures us, nature leaves the object of sexual desire undefined and its gender is imposed socially,[6] then this constitutes the strongest reason why society should socialize children towards heterosexuality and thus maximize individual happiness and social stability. The members of the Mattachine Society, when asked, agreed almost unanimously that if they had sons they would wish them to be heterosexual. They would not wish their own children to be homosexual—these people who have no children; but they would much like to make as many as possible of other people's children homosexual. "We're not afraid anymore," declares the Reverend Troy Perry; and the reason they are not afraid anymore is that they are numerous enough to be wooed by politicians and because they know how to organize for political purposes. They have, accordingly, powerful motivation for augmenting their numbers, which is to say powerful motivation for weakening the institution of the family.

Karla Jay perceives homosexual oppression as a class struggle and the oppressors as white, middle class, male-dominated heterosexuals. She regards homosexuals as the negation of heterosexuality and the nuclear family.[7] Alan Young tells us he was into fighting the pigs, but found it hard to handle the swift coming together of the personal and the political thrust upon him when he came to understand the implications of his sexual orientation. His ideas about revolution and about homosexuals are different now. Much of the energy of gay liberation, he now understands, should be directed against straight men, the legal system, the police, the church, the nuclear family, the mass media, and the psychiatric establishment. He goes on to say that being tolerated is not enough—it is only the beginning: straights must stop holding on to their straight identity. By denying homosexual love, by saying it is essentially a private matter, straights are trying to perpetuate male supremacy, sexism and anti-homosexuality. One can imagine the cries of outrage that would be heard if it were suggested to him, "You must stop holding on to your homosexual identity."

To move from the area of popular agitation to that of scholarship: a recent book by Dr. C. A. Tripp entitled *The Homosexual Matrix* bears on its dust wrapper the following encomium by Wardell Pomeroy, co-author of the Kinsey Reports:

> This is unquestionably the best book I have read on the subject of homosexuality (and I have read most of them); indeed, one that the test of time should prove great. It raises a host of new issues, and it should prove the fountainhead for engendering a generation of research—a book destined to become a classic.

High praise, and, one would suppose, from an authoritative source.[8] The back of the same dust wrapper assures us that "the book includes scores of new revelations based on solid research" including an explanation of "why birth rates are high where homosexuality is high." Interesting if true—though it would put the kibosh on the repeated claim made by homosexuals that they are acting responsibly in not bringing children into an overpopulated world—acting responsibly, that is to say, in turning over the breeding and rearing of the next generation to those they deem less responsible than themselves.[9] The "solid research" upon which the above "revelation" is based in given on page 37, where Dr. Tripp suggests that it might seem that the continuation of the race depends on heterosexuality and that homosexuality, especially rampant homosexuality, might threaten human survival. Not only is this untrue, he says, but nearly the op-

180

posite is the case: societies which suppress homosexuality generally do so with broad-based moral tenets which weaken heterosexuality more than its competition. Furthermore, he says, societies which are lenient towards homosexuality and practice it most are societies with the greatest problem of overpopulation. Now it is a matter of common knowledge that the American birthrate was at its highest during the 1950s, when homosexuality was severely repressed, and at its lowest in the Gay 70s, with homosexuals flaunting their lifestyle everywhere and with sexual impotence the commonest problem registered at campus health and counseling centers. It is a matter of common knowledge that in Germany during the Weimar era homosexuals enjoyed great freedom, and that when Hitler came to power he herded hundreds of thousands of them into concentration camps and put them to death—and launched German mothers on a program of breeding soldiers for the Reich. It is a matter of common knowledge that the Scandinavian nations have extremely low birth rates—and that they are quite tolerant of homosexuality. (One 9th-grade textbook informs Swedish schoolchildren that "homosexuality among adults is now accepted by society.") If the author of the "best book" on homosexuality can make such a mistake about facts known to everybody, the literature on this subject should obviously be read with a great deal of caution.

Tripp's scorn for psychotherapists is without bound. He believes they have had little success of any kind. People who have brought problems to therapists have had cause to regret it. They have been repudiated by science, especially by sex researchers, who shake their heads at them and despair over their nonsense. He tells of a group of Yale professors and graduate students dipping into their entertainment fund to pay a high-ranking member of the American Psychiatric Association to make a fool of himself by lecturing on Freud's theories—thus demonstrating his ignorance and the contrast between what used to be thought and what is now known.

Such professional scorn is worth emphasizing in view of the frequent appeals made to the wisdom of the psychiatric profession in acknowledging that homosexuality is "not a disease." Before this acknowledgement the homosexuals were in widespread agreement with Tripp's view. The homo-

181

sexual writer Gary Alinder thought Dr. Irving Bieber of the American Psychiatric Association was one of the worst mind-pigs. Alinder narrates how he and some of his fellow homosexuals invaded the 1970 convention of the APA and intimidated it, commandeering the microphone, telling the psychiatrists they had listened long enough, and were now in a mood to do the talking themselves, averring that it was the psychiatrists themselves who were sick whereas they, the homosexuals, were gay and proud. Alinder goes on to describe how one homosexual named Konstantin scampered about the convention in a bright red dress, how another named Andy laid it on to twenty shrinks in a Gay Liberation workshop, and how others sailed a paper airplane down from the balcony.[10] Whether in consequence of this demonstration or not, the APA in 1974 counted the heads of its mind-pigs and informed the world that the truth about homosexuality was exactly the opposite of what it had the previous year told the world to be the truth—homosexuality was OK after all. The APA and its mind-pigs were accordingly (now that they had been properly chastened) hailed as a body of learned savants whose wisdom could be appealed to. Being gay accords with recent stated realizations about the nature of human nature, David Loovis informs us. He asks himself what these realizations might be and he replies that the APA has now pronounced homosexuality to be not a mental disease, a pronouncement which was challenged but confirmed by a referendum vote. The ramifications of this recognition are, he assures us, far-reaching. In what way? Because we now understand that human sexual nature is not twisted or evil if it is homosexual—just as the greatest psychologists have always said.[11]

According to a brochure published by the National Gay Task Force Alliance, "The American Psychiatric Association no longer considers homosexuality a mental disorder. . . . An educational effort conducted by the NGTF led the APA to issue a formal, written policy that 'homosexuality *per se* does not constitute any form of mental disorder.' "

But back to Loovis. Does this APA view, he asks, mean that the old tourist, with visor, camera, wife and five kids, might be gay? Hard to believe, he says, but given the right place, time, atmosphere, and partner, that old coot might become another Oscar Wilde.

Loovis seems not to realize what he is giving away. If (1) human nature is potentially straight *and* gay, as he says, and if (2) the old coot might become gay in the right place, time, and company, then the reverse must be true: in the right place, time and company homosexuals could be "cured" and made heterosexual.

In any case, what is one to think of such a diametric reversal of opinion as that made by the APA? Why should one suppose its post-browbeating opinion is any better than its pre-browbeating one? Or that the earlier scorn for the APA by homosexuals was less justified than its present reverence for it? And why should a head count of psychiatrists at a convention be worth any more than a head count of theologians at a church council or a head count of senators voting on the Gulf of Tonkin Resolution? All but two of our senators on this latter occasion were willing to let themselves be hypnotized by the waving wizard hands of Lyndon Johnson and the soft, silken falsehoods of Dean Rusk.

Their oppression is a constant theme with homosexuals. The Radicalesbians Health Collective complains that the existing health system is geared to help the nuclear and heterosexual family, not the "personal family of those we love." One of them finds it a grievance that her father can receive blood if he needs it but her friends and lovers cannot. If these friends and lovers needed help, she would be unable to sign legal papers to admit them to a hospital. Her friends and lovers are not considered her immediate family.[12]

It doesn't occur to her that the father can get blood because he has paid for it or has previously donated blood and that her friends cannot get blood because they have not. Laws and institutions which discriminate against her and her fellow lesbians must, she thinks, be changed or abolished entirely —which is to say all props for the institution of the family must be abolished.

Heterosexuality is f____ up, declares Carl Wittman, and he adds that marriage is a contract which smothers men and women, which denies their needs, and which loads them with impossible demands. He congratulates homosexuals that

183

they have the strength to refuse the roles demanded of them. Gays, he says, may turn on to women when they want to rather than when they "should"—and that they may come to want to when women's liberation has changed the nature of heterosexual relationships,[13] meaning, evidently, when marriage and the family are destroyed.

Everybody, *including children,* say Bruce Voeller and Jean O'Leary, co-directors of the National Gay Task Force, has the right to choose private morality for themselves.[14] In other words, parents have no business socializing their children and preparing them to be responsible adults. Perhaps such socialization is the business of the indoctrinated schoolteachers Ms. O'Leary has in mind when she tells us of teachers who should be required to take courses in which lesbianism is presented in a favorable light and in which students are encouraged to explore alternative lifestyles, including lesbianism. The schools themselves should offer programs of lesbian studies, provide lesbian books, and form lesbian clubs.[15] According to the 1972 Platform of the National Coalition of Gay Organizations in Chicago, there should be federal financing of sex education courses, taught by gays, in which children would be told that homosexuality is a healthy alternative to heterosexuality. The Third World Gay Revolution of New York demands a free education system that teaches "us" our true identity and history and that presents all varieties of human sexuality without advocating any one of them. Voeller and O'Leary pose the following questions to themselves: "What you're asking for is a license to flaunt your private life in public, isn't it?" Their reply to themselves is that it is the heterosexuals who do most of the flaunting, that these people kiss and embrace one another in public, talk about their children, tell where they went last weekend with their spouses, and so forth. Evidently they believe that if Shakespeare can flaunt heterosexuality in *Romeo and Juliet,* homosexuals are equally justified in their own flaunting, as for example in San Francisco's Gay Pride parades in which the marchers chanted, "What we need is revolution," and carried placards reading "Dyke Power" and "Dyke and Faggot Anarchists," in which men in women's clothes and women in men's clothes posed for photographers, in which men appeared nude and engaged in sexual activity, in which one of

184

the marchers wore a black leather garter belt, nylon stockings, heavy leather boots, purple panties, and nothing else.[16]

To be sure, there is the prudent consideration that Anita Bryant might get hold of movies of such goings-on, as she did in 1976, and use them for propaganda purposes; and accordingly, the parade organizers in 1977 asked the drag queens to stay home and the rest of the boys to avoid their more outrageous performances—thus discriminating against them on the grounds of their sexual and affectional preference and forcing them into a conspiracy to pretend (to borrow a phrase from Voeller and O'Leary) that they don't exist. Voeller and O'Leary, incidentally, think heterosexuals are really worried that they will discover homosexuals are *not* irresponsible freaks—so there is nothing to be gained by encouraging such prejudices.

Carl Wittman laments that media and advertising falsely idealize man/woman relationships and make homosexuals wish they were different, wish they were "in." Family living classes teach children how they are supposed to turn out, he complains—a strange complaint to hear from someone who five pages earlier had said that the object of sexual desire is left undefined by nature.

He has another idea: sex with animals, which may be the beginning of interspecies communication. Such a breakthrough already has been made with dolphins. Anything, one gathers, is better than a woman.

He cites a caprophile who digs eating excrement during sex: not that he savors the taste or texture too much, but he thinks of it as symbolic of his being so far into sex that nothing bothers him. Sado-masochism is great too—a highly artistic thing.[17] He recognizes that "we" can't change "Amerika" alone and believes homosexuals must form an alliance with the feminists, the closest ally they have.[18]

The Gay Revolutionary Party Manifesto laments how in the past gay people have been unable to form alliances and, accordingly, have been forced into individual solutions such as criminality, madness, mysticism, abstract creativity, and suicide. Now things are different. There is going to be revolution, total change reaching to the roots of the social order, destroying whatever in it restrains freedom. Gay revolution will overthrow the straight male caste and other forms of sexism. Such a revolution differs from others in being a complete, rather than a partial one.[19] True, there probably will be a reactionary repression aimed to retain straightness and the family, to force women back into the home, and gay people back into the closet. This in turn would induce an insurrection by gays and feminists which would seek to do away with the power of heterosexuals. The best way of preventing reactionary repression would be for large numbers of men to become gay.[20]

The concern, it will be seen, is not to keep politics out of the bedroom, but to bring the bedroom into politics. Senator McGovern may assure us that the gay rights movement is a "struggle against prejudice and discrimination" and that "there should be no controversy in the United States over the right to personal privacy." The *New York Times* may assure us that no one should live in fear of revelations about his private life. But privacy is not the issue at this stage. The prospect of social revolution and the destruction of the sexual constitution of society are not private matters. Indeed, it is, often enough, the privacy of heterosexuals that is in question. Whose privacy is violated by, say, an advertisement in a homosexual newspaper offering to sell (for $19) a film entitled *Lockerroom!*—made with a hidden movie camera in a college gymnasium—showing "hunky jocks" showering, urinating, undressing. The movie, the seller tells us, was dangerous to film.

Dangerous to film—but not, evidently, dangerous to sell, since the seller's name and address are included in the ad itself, and since the authorities are obviously not going to do anything about this violation of the law. Hunky jocks will find politicians taking an interest in their right to privacy when hunky jocks can organize themselves politically and deliver a bloc of votes on election day comparable to that delivered by homosexual voyeurs.

Most homosexuals are not a part of the "gay rights movement" in the sense of being activists or even wanting to come out of the closet; they would prefer being left alone. Yet it is not always possible to separate politics and sexuality. *Militant* homosexuality is political through and through. There will be no real political revolution, says Jill Johnston, until all women are lesbians; and she adds that the word "lesbian" now signifies a woman with a politically revolutionary identity. One's choice of a mate is not a bedroom issue but a political act. Lesbian-feminist politics is the chief means for liberating women, says Charlotte Bunch. It threatens male supremacy at its core. When politicized and organized, it will destroy the sexist, racist, capitalist, and imperialist system.[21] According to Ti-Grace Atkinson, it is full commitment, regardless of all personal considerations, that makes lesbianism politically significant.[22] According to Rita Mae Brown, lesbians must have and soon will have a party of their own, one with which women can begin the second phase of the struggle against ten thousand years of patriarchal oppression.[23] (The reference to ten thousand years signifies a notion passed around among feminists that in prehistoric times society was matriarchal—as it will be again after the revolution.)

At a "Gay Pride Week" panel held on the campus where the present writer teaches, I collected the following snippets from various speakers: "Do something to change society. . . . Try to change society. . . . It sounds like we have no 'cause' . . . to do something to change things. . . . Just being gay isn't enough. . . . Are you interested in changing things? Political? . . . I wish gay people could do something together besides just being gay. . . . I need support. I need for people to take action to change things."

A similar series of phrases from a political flyer put out by the Stonewall Democratic Club indicates the drift of homosexuals towards politics: "Make your gay vote count! . . . Get GAY power at the polls. . . . When gay people started organizing along political lines . . . politicians have started listening. . . . to VOTE as a SOLID GAY BLOCK . . . strengthen our political clout. . . . We have developed considerable political clout . . . to maximize gay political clout. . . ."

Homosexual attorney Peter Scott informs us that what homosexuals want is to be left alone. They just ask to be allowed to express affection as heterosexuals do, without fear of losing their jobs. Scott no doubt speaks for the majority, but his attitude is hardly that of the militants. Charlotte Bunch thinks that relations between men and women are essentially political and that lesbian rejection of these relationships constitutes a defiance of the political system, a

187

way of seizing power and ending the oppression of women by men. Only those women who cut their ties to male privilege can be trusted to wage serious war against male dominance.[24]

Such is the militant-lesbian analysis of the battle of the sexes. What ought to be the patriarchal counter-analysis? Bluntly, it is this: Our society has permitted itself to engender dangerously large numbers of unattractive women. If Satan can find mischief for idle hands to perform, imagine what he can do with idle sex organs, which have always been his specialty. "The power of Satan," says the *Malleus Maleficarum*, "lies in the private parts of men"; and the substantive *men* is unquestionably common gender, including women. The foot-in-the-door bit about private acts and consenting adults is archaic. Homosexuality is a matter of profound political importance.

John Murphy thinks it unfortunate that straight people and even homosexuals themselves fail to understand homosexual politics. Straights don't understand how they oppress gays, but they had better begin to understand—and *soon*, because that oppression is about to be destroyed, and with it, the world, the diseased society that we see around us. He and his fellow militants are going to restructure the most basic sexual attitudes and the function of the family. They are going to organize a new revolutionary force and a *total* revolution. The values of lifelong monogamous marriage are no longer needed. So far from merely demanding liberty for consenting adults, laws forbidding homosexual activity between individuals *of any age* should be abolished. In sum, the liberation movement aims to destroy the white male supremacist oligarchy that controls the world. The radicals are literally up front; they cannot go back or sideways. It is necessary for them to become a new kind of people.[25]

According to Ginny Berson, lesbians are angry over their oppression by males, who have f___ them over all their lives. They will put an end to *all* oppression by ending the basic oppression of male supremacy.[26] In the words of a lesbian manifesto distributed in Barcelona, Spain, lesbians aim not at simple equality with men but at the destruction of the foundations of our society.[27] The overthrow of capitalism is too small a goal for "us," says Gloria Steinem. "It is needful to overthrow the whole f___ patriarchy."[28] According to

188

Gillean Chase, it is nobody's business whether "we" are gay or straight; but the pronoun "we" appears to exclude straights, since she goes on to speak of the fantastic anger which would result if "we" dealt with the violence done to "us" by repressive sexual codes, anger which would help destroy "the system." In other words, it is "their" wish to tear down the social system based on marriage and the family, and those who wish to retain the system are the ones who must mind their own business and refrain from interfering with the system-wrecking.

Chase thinks it no accident that family and monogamy are imposed by society, since they produce workers and stabilize production by encouraging job loyalty. This is the system she would tear down. Also, she would get rid of middle class values that define success in individualistic terms as due to personal excellence.[29]

Something must be said concerning the Wolfenden Report's phrase "consenting adults." John Murphy says that there should be no age restrictions on homosexual activity. The program of the National Coalition of Gay Organizations calls for "repeal of all laws governing the age of sexual consent."[30] A headline in the *New Times* of Boston declares, "Gentlemen Prefer Boys: 24 Men Indicted for Abuse of 70 Boys in Boston Hired-Sex Ring." Tom Reeves, 37-year-old instructor at Roxbury College, lover of a thirteen-year-old boy, has come out of his "closet within a closet" to discuss the problems of intergenerational sex. He believes we must find a way to clarify these issues for the public.[31] Bella Abzug, when she was a Congresswoman, introduced a bill providing "civil rights" for homosexuals. One of the rights was a guarantee of privacy for consenting *persons*, adults not specified. Mr. Isherwood, writing of his visits to Berlin during the Weimar era, tells us that for him Berlin meant Boys—with a capital B. He preferred boys because of their shape, their voices, their smell, and the way they moved.

Much kiddyporn is homosexual. Houston police in 1975 raided a warehouse full of it, including 15,000 color slides of boys performing homosexual acts. The first ten children admitted to Covenant House in New York, a shelter for runaways, were boys who had been paid to perform in porn films.[32] Anita Bryant says her files swell daily with materials confirming that schoolchildren are being abused by homosexual schoolteachers, scoutmasters, and porn producers: "Teacher Accused of Sex Acts with Boy Student," "Police Find Sexually Abused Children," "R.I. Sex Club Lured Juveniles with Gifts," "O.C. Teacher Held on Sex Charges," "Homosexuals Used Scout Troop," "Teacher Faces Abuse Rap," "Ex-Teachers Indicted for Lewd Acts with Boys," "Senate Shown Movie of Child Porn," "Former Scoutmaster Convicted of Homosexual Acts with Boys."[33]

According to Lloyd Martin of the Los Angeles Police Department, some 70 percent of the porn market involves young boys. The Los Angeles Times of 19 November 1976 carried a story declaring that 30,000 of the city's children, many of them runaways from other areas, were being sexually abused and exploited by some 15,000 adult males, employing every kind of perversion, including sadomasochism. A 12-year-old boy could work the streets for approximately $1,000 a day, but was obliged to give about $600 of it to his pimp. The children's ages ranged from 6 to 17, and averaged 14. They were shown pornography to excite them sexually and given narcotics to lower their inhibitions. According to Captain William J. Riddle, commander of the Juvenile Division of the Department, the problem is by no means confined to Los Angeles, though it is more prevalent there. He compares it to the narcotics problem or to a contagious disease.

A Chicago branch of a nationwide prostitution ring recruits many of its young victims in California. The Los Angeles Times tells of a New Orleans homosexual ring which operated through the Boy Scouts, trading hundreds of boy victims among older men. The New Orleans police found files, questionnaires, and letters from homosexuals seeking boys. There was evidence indicating that adult homosexual perverts had infiltrated numerous youth organizations and that their activities were more or less organized and nationwide.

To Sergeant Jackie Howell, head of the Abused Child Unit of the LAPD, the popular terms "chicken" (child victim) and "chicken hawk" (adult abuser) are inappropriate—suggesting, as they do, that what is involved is cute. She protests that these are not harmless encounters between adults, but crimes committed by child molesters against boys whose average age is 14.

Many of the children, of course, come from single-parent homes headed by mothers. Such children are the sort typically exploited in "chicken films," sexually explicit shorts selling for about $100 for use on home projectors. Different child abusers and voyeurs have different age preferences and different tastes in perversions, and the films are ordered according to the age of the victim and the kind of perversion.

The *Times* article cited understandably upset the city's homosexuals, and they, assisted by the ACLU, responded a few days later by attacking the police department's budget, accusing the department of overemphasizing vice enforcement, and discriminating against minorities and homosexuals; of wasting time in enforcing laws against victimless crimes such as prostitution, gambling, pornography, and sexual conduct between "consenting adults"; and of "leaking" information of the sexual abuse and exploitation of children for the purpose of discrediting the gay community. They did not, however, deny what was said in the article.[34]

It is well known that youth is at a premium in the homosexual subculture and a homosexual who grows old had better have a wad of money if he wishes to stay in the swim of things. *The Advocate* carries many ads like the one from a 65-year-old, plump, partly bald music lover who wishes to meet a goodlooking, blond, hairless young man between 18 and 25 for mutual friendship and action. The fees are to be arranged by the younger man.

Or there are ads such as one from a college gymnast who needs financial support to finish his education and who finds it impossible to support himself. Or such as one placed by an "attractive blond" in his late 20s, with a nice build, 5'9" tall, 135 pounds, muscular and smooth, who wants a "wealthy man." The young man insists he is sincere, affectionate, honest, and not out to use someone. He is in need of someone's assistance, someone compassionate, understanding, and desirous of helping "that special person."

The cash-nexus nature of such arrangements is indicated by Loovis, who has an imaginary interlocutor ask him what a father is supposed to do if his son falls for a man as old as himself. His advice is to do what Greek fathers did in

191

antiquity—check the old man out and see if he is a solid citizen with a bank account. In other words, exploit him if he's loaded, dump him if he's not.

Gay baths are now popular, says Loovis, baths such as the Continental Baths in New York, which have a barbershop, a food shop, other shops, and a stage where Bette Midler made her debut. The very young have made it a permanent home: they are called by the desk when it is time to go to school in the morning and provided with lunches. It's amazing, says Loovis—but not really too amazing if they make $1,000 a day hustling.

Homosexual publications assure the public again and again that most child molesters are heterosexuals. Ginny Vida complains that this fact is insufficiently reported in the media. Abigail van Buren, who, for a reason known only to herself and the nine gods, has become an apologist for homosexuals, asks her readers (as part of a quiz she gives them on homosexuality) whether it is true that homosexuals are more inclined to molest children and she assures them that the answer is they are not. Of course most child molesters are heterosexuals, because most *people* are heterosexuals. But the relevant question is not whether a child molester is more likely to be a homosexual; it is whether a homosexual is more likely to be a child molester—a very different question. The answer to the first question is, of course, no; but the answer to the second is yes. John Rechy cites statistics from the *Los Angeles Times* of 28 October 1973 showing that "only" 20 percent of pedophiles are homosexuals. He imagines himself to be providing proof for his view that homosexuals are maligned as child molesters when heterosexual molesting is far, far more common. But if 20 percent of the molesting is done by exclusive homosexuals, as Rechy and the *Times* indicate, and if we accept Kinsey's statistic that exclusive homosexuals constitute only some 4 percent of the population, it follows that homosexuals are five times as likely to be child molesters as are heterosexuals.[35]

It is in this tendentious and propagandistic fashion that the present subject is generally handled. Homosexual literature assures us that Aristole, Cellini, Michelangelo, da Vinci, Shakespeare, and Milton were all known homosexuals, though such identifications are either very doubtful or certainly untrue.[36]

192

One complaint commonly heard is that society's props for marriage in the form of tax benefits and better health insurance rates deny to homosexuals benefits which in justice they are entitled to. Thus, one John Cohan, a lawyer residing in Hollywood, compares society's refusal to sanction homosexual "marriage" to the miscegenation laws of the Old South. He declares that such marriage is a fundamental right since it bestows substantial legal, social, and psychological benefits.

This man of the law seems not to have noticed that much of his argument would apply equally well to marriages with dogs, cats, and teddy bears. A man who marries his dog is not entitled to the tax benefits which society awards to heterosexual marriage, because he is not helping to stabilize society and not undertaking responsibility for the protection and rearing of the next generation. Moreover, society cannot assure a homosexual couple that their "marriage" has the same kind of validity, dignity, and significance as a heterosexual marriage without at the same time assuring heterosexuals that their marriages have no more validity and significance than sodomitical relationships. Married heterosexuals live longer and have fewer accidents: it is for this excellent reason that they have lower insurance rates. (See some of the statistics in the first chapter of Gilder's *Naked Nomads*.)

What Cohan's proposal amounts to is that a homosexual "family" consisting of two adults with two incomes and no children to support is entitled as a matter of justice to claim it has been unfairly discriminated against if it is not awarded the same tax advantages as a single income family which does undertake to support children. Such a position clearly undercuts one of the few remaining props of the family.

A somewhat similar confusion is to be found in the opinion of Norman Podhoretz, editor of a respected journal of opinion and a man capable of writing sense on most topics. He discusses the homosexual writer James Baldwin and his view that love is the greatest of all values and that sex is the most natural expression of love. It follows that the stifling of impulses towards homosexual expression of this love is unnatural—a warping of instinct which may destroy the capacity for all sexual expression whatever.

Such might be the homosexual's rationalization of his

lifestyle. Here would be the bestialist's: Do you love your dog and do you believe that sex is the most natural expression of love? Then you must realize that the stifling of your own impulses towards a sexual articulation of the love you feel for animals signifies a warping of the instincts and of the body that may end by destroying your capacity for any sexual expression whatever. Here is the adulterer's rationalization: Do you love your neighbors? Then you should commit adultery with them and hold swinging neighborhood parties. Here is the necrophiliac's rationalization: Did you love your grandmother? Then you should open her tomb and have sexual intercourse with her cadaver. Do you love your children? Then you should commit incest with them. And so on. Anything in Krafft-Ebing's *Psychopathia Sexualis* can be justified by this kind of reasoning, reasoning which has as its basis the idea that our instincts need not be channeled and disciplined.

Laziness is natural. Cowardice is natural. Lechery is natural. Wrath is natural. If these impulses are not controlled biologically, they need to be controlled by socialization and the institutions of society. Jill Johnston tells us that the mere existence of homosexuals is a threat to marriage and family, which everyone is conditioned to believe is the true way, whereas being gay means being roleless.[37] Kinsey agreed about the effect of social conditioning and he contended that the stability of heterosexual marriage depended more on custom than on love and shared experience. He believed that the rarity of permanent homosexual relationships was to be attributed to the absence of this conditioning. He thought that heterosexual relationships would be eroded if such social custom and legal props were removed.

In the same way, the homosexual contention that their lifestyle is not "catchy" flies in the face of what is known about the effect of social restraints in other matters. We had heterosexual teachers and their lifestyle didn't affect "us," they argue—which is true enough if "us" refers only to the writers, but can they give the same assurance if "us" refers also to their former classmates, some of whom may have been what William Rapsberry calls "either-way kids"? You had homosexual teachers, whether you knew it or not, they

194

argue, and they didn't affect your lifestyle. No; one or a few homosexual teachers will not influence a child, especially if they remain closeted and do not challenge the heterosexual consensus of society. But it is precisely this heterosexual consensus that militant homosexuals wish to destroy on the grounds that it discriminates against them. It is well-known that homosexuality is more common in some groups than in others, for example among Indian Moslems than among Indian Hindus. The explanation can hardly be anything other than the "social custom" to which Kinsey refers.

The Third World Gay Revolution Group of New York demands the right of self-determination for Third World people and homosexuals and the control of what they call their destinies, without which, they aver, they cannot be free. They demand free sex-change operations, free dress, free adornments. These "basic human rights" are now denied to them by the existing system which favors heterosexuality. They demand free contraceptives and contraceptive information, free 24-hour child care centers, which they themselves will control and others will pay for. They demand the abolition of the bourgeois nuclear family, free education which teaches them their true identity and history, and teaches the nature of all kinds of sexuality without advocating any one of them, such as heterosexual marriage and the family. They demand that sex role socialization be eliminated from the schools; that language should be modified to remove its sex biases; that they be given free and decent housing; the abolition of the existing judicial system, and the custom of having homosexuals tried by juries of heterosexuals rather than by juries of their homosexual peers. They demand release of homosexual prisoners, the abolition of the penal system and the police. They demand exemption of Third World and gay men from military service, an end to all institutional religions, the creation of a new society, free food, free shelter, free clothing, free transportation, free health care, free utilities, free art for all. Free, free, free—all these basic human rights.[38]

According to a homosexual cited by Karlen, the biggest hang-up with gay people is that they are all "children." Homosexuals, says May Romm, have given up hope of being accepted by parents or society, and are basically unhappy because normal family life can never be theirs. Their pretense that they are "gay" is, she thinks, a defense against the emptiness, coldness, and futility of their existence.

What sort of person, one wonders, would buy an S & M recording of Fist Goodbody's Traveling Torture Show—which we are assured is not a dramatization, not a simulation, but the real sweaty S & M performance itself from the first gasp to the last gurgle. The ad is accompanied by a photo of "Fist" himself, naked to the waist, wearing a platinum blond wig which curls down over his chest, with platinum blond eyebrows pasted over his own, a heavy chain around his neck, his face bedaubed with mascara and lipstick, wearing fingernail polish and perhaps false eyelashes, holding a coiled bullwhip in his right hand.

What are we to make of such homosexual greening of America? The tax-supported IWY conference that met in Houston in November of 1977 passed a "Sexual Preference Resolution" which included the following:

> State legislatures should enact legislation that would prohibit consideration of sexual or affectional orientation as a factor in any judicial determination of child custody or visitation rights. Rather, child custody cases should be evaluated solely on the merits of which party is the better parent, without regard to that person's sexual and affectional orientation.

Nothing is said, *nota bene,* about private acts and consenting adults. If your preferences run to public nudity and buggering, this is no concern of a judge in hearing a custody case.

It needs to be understood that the compulsiveness which is so grotesque in the context of homosexuality makes excellent sense in the context of heterosexual marriage. Consider. In no other mammalian species than homo sapiens does the male play a role fully comparable in importance with that of the female in the rearing of the young (though many male birds play an important role too). And homo sapiens is both the most successful and the most sexy of all species. Now at the same time that natural selection was making mankind, especially its males, so concupiscent, it was eliminating the female's oestrous cycle. In other species, the female is receptive to the sexual advances of the male only at those limited times when she is most likely to be fertile; but in the human species, the female is receptive at any time that she does not have a headache, so that the male lives in what might be described as a constant state of rutting. But though he is far sexier than necessary for purposes of procreation, he is not at all sexier than he needs to be for the purpose of keeping him dancing attendance upon his female and thus providing security for her and for their offspring, so that, as discussed in Chapter III, the young can enjoy a prodigiously longer infancy and childhood ("neoteny") which enables them to remain educable for up to two decades or more, and indeed, to carry their educability into adulthood and old age.

This marvelous arrangement, which not only makes women dependent upon men, but makes men willing that they should be, is now under attack by feminists, who complain that women will never be liberated until they achieve economic independence from men—which is to say, until the male provider role is destroyed, as it already largely has been in the ghettos, with the obvious consequences. With the help of the legal profession and of bureaucrats and other father-substitutes, they are well along the road to what they deem success—with the male being expected to finance this "liberation" by making alimony and child support payments and contributing the taxes which make him superfluous—except as a taxpayer. Then monogamy can be discarded and then, as Rita Mae Brown would have it, "we"—lesbians—can cure the diseases of imperialism and death that result from male dominance, and form women's collectives which will usher in the Woman's Revolution.[39]

No doubt there will soon be demands that such collectives be government supported, in order that these women may be "independent," may suckle at the public's teats, and have their hands held by bureaucrats. With women subject to male control, she thinks, men will never change; but if women withdraw their support men will have to change.

A very interesting change it would be, one Ms. Brown might inspect for herself in the ghettos of our cities—pro-

197

vided she takes a German shepherd dog with her. How different things look to those women who really are oppressed. "Now, here's how it is," declares a group of black women. "Poor black men won't support their families, won't stick with their women—all they think about is the street, dope and liquor, women . . . and their cars. That's all that counts."[40] It is to this that feminism would lead white women.

Both homosexuals and the father-substitutes in the welfare and other bureaucracies share with feminists a common interest in accelerating the present rush towards sexual suicide, since their numbers and many of their jobs depend on illegitimacy, delinquency, sexual confusion, and the destruction of the family. The more that fathers are displaced as heads of families, the greater the need for bureaucrats to rescue women and children. The more fatherless children there are, the more dependent and weak people there will be, people clamoring to be cared for by Big Brother.

The normal and socially useful channel for male sexuality, marriage and family living, has been blocked for so many males by so many difficulties, the divorce courts in particular, that men in enormous numbers have been driven to find other outlets for their sexuality and to refuse to undertake the responsibilities of marriage demanded by Malinowski's Legitimacy Principle. This refusal in turn augments the problems which drove them to the refusal in the first place. "Love," says Gilder,

> performs its most indispensable role in inducing males to submit to female cycles of sexuality. In a civilized society men ultimately must overcome the limited male sexual rhythms of tension and release, erection and ejaculation, and adopt a sexual mode responsive to the extended female pattern—proceeding through pregnancy, childbirth, and nurture. By involving the long period of bearing and nurturing children, the female pattern entails a concern for the future, a sense of growth and evolution, a need for deferring gratifications, a desire for durable and secure relationships. The male pattern naturally focuses on actively wresting pleasures

from the immediate environment. But in civilized societies, the majority of the men have come to recognize that it is the female time-orientation and the family that offer the highest rewards.

. . . .

Without a durable relationship with a woman, a man's sexual life is a series of brief and temporary exchanges, impelled by a desire to affirm his most rudimentary masculinity. But with love, sex becomes refined by selectivity, and other dimensions of personality are engaged and developed. The man himself is refined, and his sexuality becomes not a mere impulse but a meaningful commitment in society, possibly to be fulfilled in the birth of specific children legally and recognizably his. His sex life then can be conceived and experienced as having specific long-term importance like a woman's.

The man thus can integrate his immediate physical sensations with his highest aspirations for meaning and community. The sex act itself can become a civilizing human affirmation, involving his entire personality and committing it, either in fact or in symbol, to a long-term engagement in a meaningful future.

All these aspects of love must be present for the highest erotic experience: choice, desire, and aspiration. Sexual desire alone fails to lead men to make durable choices; it fails to evoke aspirations for the future. Copulation itself is focused on the present. Choice is required and aspirations are evoked chiefly by the conscious or unconscious desire to have children with a specific partner. This is the key to love.[41]

Feminism and our divorce laws have made such love and responsibility too costly for tens of millions of men and are producing a society of men and women incapable of love and commitment. Our traditional guilt culture is breaking down into a rudimentary shame culture.[42] Ethical values are being abandoned or relativized. If one enjoys himself, says Peter

Fisher in *The Gay Mystique*,[43] he has as good a lifestyle as any. Illegitimacy has doubled since the mid-1960s. More than half of black infants are illegitimate. IQs are plummeting. Crude supersitions—astrology, witchcraft, voodoo—are becoming commonplace. "Individuality" has lost any reference to integrity and now signifies little more than petulance. Institutions of higher learning have become propaganda mills for Marxism, feminism, and homosexuality.[44] Administrators and politicians have, in order to survive, adopted a practice of buying off their most clamorous and immature constituents by making excessive demands on the mature, responsible, and hardworking ones. Sex is increasingly regarded in terms of the Playboy-feminist-homosexual philosophy that its purpose is fun and games, having little relevance to the stability of society or the fundamental unit of which society is composed, the family.

It is now necessary to consider what responsible people ought to do about the present chaotic situation.

Notes

1. David Loovis, *Straight Answers About Homosexuality for Straight Readers*. Englewood Cliffs, N.J., 1977, p. 25.

2. Quoted in *The Anita Bryant Story*, p. 113.

3. *The Advocate*, 19 April 1978.

4. Dr. Frank Beach knows of no authenticated instance of male or female animals preferring homosexual partners—if by homosexual is meant complete sexual relations, including climax. He acknowledges that there is mounting of males by males, but without intromission of the penis or climax. There is likewise mounting of females by females, which is admittedly homosexual in the literal and descriptive sense that it is male-to-male and female-to-female behavior. But to call it homosexual in the human sense would be, he says, "an interpretation." He even doubts whether "mounting ought to be regarded as sexual." See Karlen's *Sexuality and Homosexuality*, p. 399.

According to Karlen, the evidence suggests that we should abandon the notions of biologically rooted bisexuality and latency. (p. 396) He says there is no homosexuality among birds. Males do not copulate and the "triumph rite" and pairing of ganders, spoken of by Lorenz, involve no copulation. Mammals in their natural state—probably even in captivity—perform no homosexual acts. (pp. 391f)

5. Anne Koedt, when asked how she was able to overcome her heterosexual training and allow her feelings to come out, replied that it could never have happened without the existence of the Women's Movement. ("Can Women Love Women?"—interview by Anne Koedt)

According to Robin Morgan (*Ms.*, September 1975), many anti-lesbian women conquered the feelings of threat and terror and "came out," *learning* proudly to love other women.

According to a homosexual named "Fred" quoted by Karlen (p. 159), most homosexuals could be heterosexual if they wanted to live responsibly.

According to Kinsey (*Sexual Behavior in the Human Male*, p. 663), some homosexuals change from exclusively heterosexual patterns and vice versa.

According to Simone de Beauvoir, homosexuality is a chosen preference, at once motivated and deliberately adopted. (*Second Sex*, p. 424)

6. "A Gay Manifesto," in *Out of the Closets: Voices of Gay Liberation*, p. 331.

7. *Ibid.*, p. 1.

8. It should perhaps be mentioned that Drs. Pomeroy and Tripp appear to be friends.

9. The claim that it is responsible to be homosexual and not have children is, of course, incompatible with the claim that homosexuality is innate, like left-handedness, and cannot be changed.

10. Len Richmond and Gary Noguera, *Los Angeles Free Press*, 14 August 1970, reprinted in *The Gay Liberation Book*, p. 107.

11. *Ibid.*, p. 25.

12. *Out of the Closets*, p. 122.

13. *Ibid.*, p. 331.

14. *Los Angeles Times*, 12 June 1977.

15. Quoted in *Christian, Be Watchful*, pp. 13, 20.

16. Details from *Los Angeles Times*, 27 June 1977.

17. *Out of the Closets*, p. 338.

18. *Ibid.*, p. 340.
19. *Lesbianism in the Women's Movement*, p. 35.
20. *Ibid.*, p. 77.
21. *Out of the Closets*, p. 344.
22. In Johnston, *Lesbian Nation: The Feminist Solution*, p. 276.
23. *Lesbianism in the Women's Movement.* Baltimore, Diana Press, 1975, p. 77.
24. *Ibid.*, pp. 29ff.
25. *Homosexual Liberation*, p. 175.
26. *Lesbianism in the Women's Movement*, p. 17.
27. *Off Our Backs*, 4 February 1978.
28. *Michigan Free Press*, 15 April 1974; quoted in *Christian, Be Watchful*, p. 10.
29. *The Other Woman*, September/October 1976.
30. Cited in *The Anita Bryant Story*, p. 90.
31. *Seven Days*, 19 May 1978.
32. *Human Events*, 7 January 1978.
33. *The Anita Bryant Story*, p. 89.
34. *Los Angeles Times*, 24 November 1976.
35. Other instances of Abby's casuistry in justifying homosexuality could be given. Dr. Irving Bieber estimates the number of exclusive homosexuals at one to two percent, which would make them ten to twenty times as likely to be child molesters. Petropinto and Simenauer, *Beyond the Male Myth*, p. 63, estimated exclusive homosexuals at 1.3 percent of the population.
36. See Karlen, pp. 38, 108.
37. *Lesbian Nation: The Feminist Solution*, p. 187.
38. *Out of the Closets*, ed. Karla Jay and Allen Young, pp. 363ff.
39. *Lesbianism in the Women's Movement*, p. 67.
40. *Ibid.*, p. 74.
41. *Sexual Suicide*, pp. 36f.
42. A shame culture is guided not by an internalized conscience but by what one supposes others are thinking about him. See Ruth Benedict's *The Chrysanthemum and the Sword* and E. R. Dodd's *The Greeks and The Irrational* for useful examinations of these two kinds of culture.
43. Page 208.
44. Cynthia Secor (*Change*, February 1975) expresses

satisfaction that gay organizations and caucuses and a number of books advocating homosexuality published by major presses have created a climate in which homosexuals now feel it is safe to organize.

XII

The Last Liberation

The central role will forever belong to women; they set the rhythm of things.
—Steven Goldberg

ALL SOCIETIES ARE run, and must be run, by males. There are a number of reasons why this is so—greater male aggression and superior male ability in the handling of abstractions being two. A less obvious but more basic reason is that males have a sexual inferiority complex that makes it necessary for them to find some kind of compensatorily meaningful activity which can give them assurance that they are just as important as women. Otherwise they run amok.

Societies are run primarily for the benefit of women and children, but women and children are no more to be trusted to run societies directly than the passengers in the back seat of a taxi are to be trusted to directly handle the controls of the vehicle that is operated for their benefit. The ghettos are the obvious example of societies that fail to find ways of utilizing male aggression, and they are kept from capsizing only by subventions from the male-run society on the outside.

The problems of these ghettos, thanks to feminism and government interference and mismanagement, are becoming the problems of the larger society. Enormous as these problems are, they are not at all complex or difficult to solve if we will but address ourselves resolutely to them. It will be useful to epitomize what needs to be done.

Most important, society must preserve and strengthen its basic unit, the nuclear, patriarchal family. It must do this primarily by abolishing the system of welfare that subsidizes and encourages illegitimacy, and by abolishing alimony and child-support payments that subsidize and encourage divorce. Feminists who clamor about the injustice of the nuclear family on the grounds that it makes women economically dependent upon men should be given exactly what they demand—economic independence. Economic independence does not mean economic dependence, direct or indirect, that permits women to subsist through ex-husbands, welfare, and bureaucratic largesse such as free child care and affirmative action programs. It means competition on the basis of equal opportunity, with men and women being evaluated on the basis of merit alone.

The elimination of alimony and child-support payments will mean, as has been pointed out in Chapter II, that the earning power of the parents will be an important consideration in determining the custody of children in a divorce case. This will normally mean paternal custody and paternal occupancy of the family dwelling. The benefits of this arrangement are obvious. There will be fewer divorces; the family and society itself will be stabilized; crime, delinquency, illegitimacy, sexual confusion, and much of the other social pathology associated with the fatherless family will decline.

The continuing subsidization of ex-wives by ex-husbands is not merely unjust, it is silly. Alimony is virtually unknown outside of America and Europe. "The obtaining of alimony has become almost an industry . . . especially in America," wrote Theodore Besterman in 1934. Besterman should be living at this hour. Alimony and child-support payments often impoverish men to the point where they cannot afford remarriage, or they compel second wives to work to support first wives.[1] According to Robert Wernick, "Some divorced women demand huge payments, not so much out of greed, Willard Waller has suggested, but in an attempt to make it economically impossible for their former husbands to remarry. And since alimony ceases on the recipient's remarriage, a divorcée has a financial incentive to remain single, prolonging both the payments and her husband's inability to afford a new marriage."[2]

"The reasonable needs of a wife commensurate with her station in life are a circumstance the court should consider in determining a just and reasonable amount of her support," we are informed by the Honorable J. Ashley of the Fifth Division of the Second Appellate District of the Court of Appeals of the State of California. But the Honorable J. Ashley is quite aware that the woman to whom he refers is not a "wife." She is an ex-wife. She has in all probability abandoned her marriage and she performs no services for her husband. Her "station in life" was a station conferred upon her by the status and largesse of her ex-husband. And according to the reasoning of the Honorable J. Ashley, the more magnanimous her ex-husband was to her in the past, the more that ex-husband deserves to be punished by the divorce court over which J. Ashley presides. A more tortured piece of reasoning would be difficult to find, even in the fairyland created by the legal profession. It's called equal rights *for women*.

"If you get away from the word alimony," declares the feminist lawyer Diane Blank, "the concept is a fair one,"[3] a deferred compensation for the wife's contributions to the home, she thinks—a deferred compensation to which the husband, however, is not entitled for *his* contributions to the home. For the greater the husband's contributions have been, the more he is to be punished rather than rewarded by the J. Ashleys of the legal profession.

According to another lawyer, Emily Goodman, the husband "acquires a profession, affluence, status and, most important, future income which she will not be part of—and no one will compensate her for the loss of education."[4]

No; she will "not be a part of his future income"—not if she divorces him, and if there are no J. Ashleys to rescue her and punish her ex-husband for being guilty of "no fault." But suppose that society removed its J. Ashleys from the bench if they refused to keep the oaths of office that require them to administer impartial justice—to men as well as to women. What then would be the situation in a county like the county of Los Angeles, where J. Ashley interprets the law, and where 95 percent of divorces are filed by women? In such a county, and under such circumstances, a woman might wish to remain "a part of his future income" by not getting a divorce.

Alimony is a disincentive for a woman either to work or to remarry. "The cocktail lounges of America are filled with unhappy, lonely, frustrated, and alcoholic women," says Judge Alton Pfaff.[5] "I could marry him if I wanted to," writes a reader to Abigail van Buren, "but if I did I would lose the alimony I'm getting from my last husband and also the child support from my kid's father (my second husband). I also think marriage is very old-fashioned today."[6]

Old-fashioned indeed, like most of the best customs; but it must seem especially old-fashioned to someone like the woman quoted, who, thanks to the J. Ashleys of the judiciary, already has a male strapped into his milking-machine and who can compel him to submit to involuntary servitude for the rest of his natural life. "Once," to quote Jeanne Cambrai, "is enough" for her.

According to the economist Elisabeth Landers, "Business partners make an investment on the assumption that it will work. If it doesn't, parties should be compensated for the investment they made."[7] She refers to divorce.

Observe Little Mr. Compensator hiding behind the passive voice in Landers' phrase "should be compensated." Little Mr. Compensator is the male-chauvinist-pig-oppressor-husband who has been victimizing his wife by paying her bills and thus making her dependent, which is bad. If he wants to be good, he ought to pay his ex-wife's bills and thus make her independent. "The *parties* should be compensated," says Landers, and the plural of the noun I have italicized shows that she is not just thinking of women, as does her further comment: "Alimony serves as a kind of insurance policy to protect the investments made *by the couple* in the event of divorce. . . ." It would be cruel to describe anything this naive as an attempt to deceive.

"Alimony means back pay—for the woman's contribution as homemaker to the family," says Cynthia Brown Morse of the National Organization for Women[8]—as though a man's providing for his family were not a contribution but an imposition for which he owed indemnities. Say rather that alimony means retroactive punishment for the folly of a male foolish enough to have placed himself in a position where the petulance of a woman, the avarice of lawyers, and the moral insensitivity of a judge can combine to destroy the motives that make him a useful member of society.

The custom of the husband's paying the wife's attorney's fees must be done away with. A lawyer faced with the dubious prospect of trying to collect a fee from a woman is far more likely to offer socially useful advice about buying a new nightgown than he is to cooperate in the wrecking of a family. A woman faced with personal fiscal responsibility for her adventures is far more likely to accept the socially useful advice than to make a choice that will not only cost her her husband's paycheck but also confront her with the covetousness of the legal profession. In any case it is morally repugnant to compel a man to finance the destruction of his own family.

Families headed by fathers do not go on welfare. They do not create the social pathology we see everywhere. This pathology is created by fatherless families, which society is subsidizing at an unprecedented and increasing rate. Alimony and child support are the only surviving relics of the detestable practice of imprisonment for debt—and of a debt that society has no moral right or practical reason to impose, and that an ex-husband has no moral obligation to pay. "They can literally leave you in jail until you figure a way to pay up," writes Charles Metz. "Obviously this is frequently a losing game—except for the wife. What she doesn't collect from you in money she can collect in revenge. Also, under these circumstances she can collect full AFDC. AFDC pays very regularly and, in some cases, very well. Some courts will allow you about $1.50 a day for every day you spend in jail. This can be applied to your back payments."[9] Courts will even enforce upon husbands the requirement of reimbursing AFDC for payments it has made to ex-wives who have kidnapped children from ex-husbands who have legal custody of them. Incredible but true.

It is a matter of national economic necessity, as well as common sense, to get rid of the subsidization of the present wretched state of affairs which is creating so many fatherless families and forcing cities and counties to the verge of bankruptcy. Illegitimate children must be placed for adoption in two-parent families where they have a reasonable chance to lead happy and useful lives. Children of divorce must normally be placed in the custody of fathers. *Families headed by fathers don't go on welfare.* They pay their own way. And they are far more likely to produce useful citizens. For every fatherless family on AFDC there exists a demoralized male who has been deprived of his role as provider for and head of a family. And within a year of the birth of an illegitimate AFDC child, one out of four of the mothers of such children is pregnant again.[10]

It must be emphasized that abolishing the subsidization of fatherless families by welfare and child-support payments will benefit women in the way they can best be benefited—by strengthening marriage and the family—putting economic advantages on the side of these institutions instead of pitting them against them.

Study after study has demolished the myth that a child needs a mother more than it needs a father; and no study is needed—only a pair of eyes—to see that the pathology of our society is related to fatherless families. The importance of fathers is shown, if by nothing else, by the cost of the bureaucracies intended to replace them and to rectify the damage done to society by their absence from increasing millions of families. The solution is as obvious as the sun—stop subsidizing the destruction of families. All that is lacking is the determination to apply this solution.

A movement for men's rights must give high priority to reforming the legal profession. Men must be guaranteed the same rights as women. Dialogues such as the following must no longer be tolerated:

Wife's Attorney: What is your name, please?
Wife: Mrs. Mary Smith.
Wife's Attorney: And what is your place of residence, Mrs. Smith?
Wife: Las Vegas, Nevada.
Wife's Attorney: And how long have you lived in Las Vegas, Nevada?
Wife: Six weeks.

Wife's Attorney: And do you intend to make Las Vegas, Nevada your permanent place of residence?
Wife: Yes, I do.

Such is the law that the law-and-order boys tell us we must respect. Such is the law that we must change. The currently fashionable substitute for this charade—no fault divorce—has been discussed in Chapter II. It represents perhaps the only alteration of the earlier system capable of revealing the character of the legal profession in a more pitiable light. The earlier system established the husband's extreme cruelty by having the wife commit perjury and by requiring the judge to pretend that he believed her perjury and that he was therefore justified in depriving the husband of his children, his home, his property, and his income. The procedure was so palpably dishonest and cruel that even the legal profession was embarrassed to perform it, and it accordingly reformed the system by imposing the same penalties upon the husband because he was guilty of no fault. The time has arrived for men to insist that the corollary of no fault is no punishment.

A Men's Liberation movement must oppose programs for free child care, programs that constitute subsidization of the institution of the fatherless family, of women at the expense of men, and of two-income families at the expense of one-income families. Betty Friedan, in arguing the feminist case in favor of such programs, tells us that "for women to have full human identity and freedom, they must have economic independence." As indicated previously, this feminist position ought to be exactly the position of a Men's Liberation movement as well: let liberated women be economically independent *by not being subsidized.*

Men's Liberation must work to restore the rational socialization of children, now being perverted by the feminists who are acquiring such powerful influence in educational institutions, including higher education. Such socialization requires that boys and girls be steered away from competition with each other and towards goals that will maximize their chances for success and happiness. For girls, this means emphasizing the central importance of maternity and the family. Feminist attempts to downgrade this central function

210

of society in the interest of career elitism need to be understood as attempts by these women to be revenged upon society for their unattractiveness.

Our society must revive the ancient courtship customs of our wise ancestors, customs that permit the female to arouse the sexual passions of the male, but which prohibit her from having sexual intercourse with him prior to marriage, so that the male returns home from his Saturday night date aching and yearning to possess the body of his beloved, but knowing that he cannot do so unless he gets a job, earns an honest living, becomes a useful member of society, and undertakes a lifelong commitment to love, honor, and protect his wife and children. The correlative responsibility on the part of the woman must be her undertaking to love, honor, *and obey* her husband, so that the husband, when he undertakes his heavy responsibility for his family, has an assurance that he cannot be deprived of his children and his property by female petulance and legalistic chicane.

Men's Liberation must emphasize the twin principles of subsidiarity and patriarchy. Subsidiarity means that decision-making should take place at the lowest possible level. Things should not be decided in Washington if they can be decided in City Hall, and they should not be decided in City Hall if they can be decided within the family. Patriarchy means that the husband is the head of the family. Both of these principles are correctly understood by feminists as maximizing the decision-making power of husbands and fathers; and both are therefore denounced by the feminists, who much prefer to have decisions made by bureaucrats and politicians whom they can pressure and manipulate. The transference of decision making to such bureaucrats and politicians and the increasing number of alliances between feminists and government are two of the principal causes of the present erosion of the family and of the father's role within it—and of the strengthening of the obnoxious bureaucracies that have come to play such an enormous and growing part in our lives.

The most essential step in establishing subsidiarity and patriarchy is tax reform. The abuses committed with our tax money are so notorious that they need not be discussed. It is common knowledge that the subsidization of Congressmen's mistresses is one of the very best purposes for which this money is used.

Californians in June of 1978 showed the way to tax reform—and showed that such reform is quite simple. But though the property taxes slashed by the Californians were indeed obnoxious and oppressive, the income tax is a far greater evil. The goal of tax reform—whether by tax avoidance, barter, credits, the formation of guilds and churches whose members perform services for each other without an exchange of money, or the endowing of foreign charities headquartered in foreign banks—is to enable citizens to spend their own money rather than having it spent wastefully and irresponsibly by bureaucrats, who, for the most part, use it not to provide services for citizens but to inflict grievous disservices upon these citizens. All that is required to reform these abuses is a resolute determination to implement the reform.

In addition to the foregoing program for Men's Liberation, one additional proposal might be considered. This is for American men to do what Alexander the Great and his generals did—marry foreign women. Consider the following ad which appeared recently in *Psychology Today:*

JAPANESE GIRLS MAKE WONDERFUL WIVES. We have large number of listings. Many interested in marriage. Only $1.00 brings application, photos, names, descriptions, questionnaire, etc. Japan International, Box 156-PT, Carnelian Bay, California 95711.

This same ad has appeared frequently in *Moneysworth,* from which the following were taken:

More than two thousand women from all over the world responded to a full page "Wife Wanted" ad by Bob Kemper of North Miami. . . .

Beautiful Mexican Girls. Correspondence. Dtls, photos, $1, Latins, Box 1716, Chula Vista, CA 92012.

212

According to the *Los Angeles Times* of 17 March 1976,

> Virtually all over the world, there are long lines of
> people in front of U.S. Consulates, people willing to
> give almost anything for permission to live in the
> United States.

According to Kurganoff's *Women in the USSR,* in the Soviet
Union "among people over 33 years of age . . . there are 170
women per 100 men. These superfluous women . . . 19 million
of them, have no chance to marry and have a home or family.
. . . Soviet sociologists emphasize as a great achievement,
that in Moscow over 50 percent of families have their own
bathrooms, natural gas, and telephone. In Gorky and Ivanovo
the availability of such community services is as yet more
limited."

The fact is that there are scores of millions of women in the
world who know all about the way American men pamper
their women, who perhaps make little jokes about it, but who
would very much like to be on the receiving end of some of the
"oppression" about which our arrogant feminists clamor.
The organizing of a matrimonial service which would bring
American men and foreign women together might be developed into a profitable undertaking capable of subsidizing a
program of men's liberation.

The ills of the ghetto are becoming the ills of the larger society—with the important difference, however, that the larger
society lacks the ghetto's resource of being able to perpetuate
its condition by laying a guilt-trip on Whitey which can be
used for panhandling purposes. What these ills are can be
easily understood by anyone with the imagination required
to put himself inside the head of a twelve-year-old black boy
who lives in a ghetto tenement where toilets fall through the
ceiling, where junkies sleep in corridors between piles of
excrement, where all visible positions of responsibility are
occupied by females, and where he hears his fourteen-year-
old sister explain to his mother (he has no father) that since
all her girlfriends are having babies, she too intends to get
pregnant, to drop out of junior high school, to go on welfare
and to be given a pad of her own. What the twelve-year-old
boy understands with great clarity is that there are few

213

places in society in which he has any reasonable prospect of earning a useful living and having a family of his own.

There is a wisdom embedded in the language we speak, which is nowhere better illustrated than in the expletives we use to heap abuse upon our enemies. A bastard is a child who has no father. A slut or bitch is a female of a lower order whose designation is properly transferred to a female of our own species who is conspicuous for sexual promiscuity or nastiness of disposition. A son-of-a-bitch is a male whose position in society cannot be indicated in terms of his relationship to his father, like Tom's son, Will's son, John's son, Fitz-Gerald, Gom-ez and Mac-Donald, but must instead be indicated in terms of his relationship to the aforementioned slut or bitch. We shall have to decide soon whether we wish to be a society of bastards, sluts, bitches, and sons-of-bitches, because that is what we are rapidly becoming, thanks to the destruction of the patriarchal family by feminists, bureaucrats, and the legal profession.

NOTES

1. Some of the horror stories collected by R. F. Doyle in *The Rape of the Male*, pp. 93ff., are almost unbelievable.
2. *The Family*, p. 137.
3. *Pasadena Star-News*, 22 February 1976.
4. *Ibid.*
5. Metz, *Divorce and Custody for Men*, p. 69.
6. *Los Angeles Times*, 21 August 1977.
7. *Los Angeles Times*, 28 August 1977.
8. *U.S. News and World Report*, 12 September 1977.
9. Metz, p. 50.
10. *U.S. News and World Report*, 6 June 1978.

Index

215

Wittman, Carl, 179, 183-184, 185
Wolfenden Report, 189
Woman and the Family, 141
Women: affirmative action for, 98-133; complaints of oppression by, 91-93, 94-97; and confusion caused by feminism, 130-131; discrimination against, 104, 123-124, 132; pampered existence of, 93-94; and status, 128-129

Women in the USSR, 213
Women's Survival Catalogue, 138
Wyland, Francie, 120-122
Wylie, Philip, 71-72, 82-83
Wysor, Bettie, 163

Young, Alan, 179-180